CONTEMPORARY THEATRE REVIEW
AN INTERNATIONAL JOURNAL

Aims and Scope

Contemporary Theatre Review is an international journal concerned with all aspects of theatre – from text-based drama and current developments worldwide, to work of an interdisciplinary or cross-cultural nature. The journal includes primary material, production notes, documents and interviews as well as research. **Contemporary Theatre Review** complements the companion **Contemporary Theatre Studies** book series.

Notes for contributors can be found at the back of the journal.

© 1998 OPA (Overseas Publishers Association) Amsterdam B.V. Published under license under the Harwood Academic Publishers imprint, part of The Gordon and Breach Publishing Group. All rights reserved.

Reprinted 2004
by Routledge,
2 Park Square, Milton Park, Abingdon, Oxon, OX14 4RN

Transferred to Digital Printing 2004

World Wide Web Addresses

Additional information is also available through the Publisher's web home page site at http://www.gbhap.com. Full text on-line access and electronic author submissions may also be available.

Editorial enquiries by e-mail: <editlink@gbhap.com>.

Ordering Information

Four issues per volume. Subscription are renewed on an annual basis. 1997 Volume(s): 6–8

Orders may be placed with your usual supplier or at one of the addresses shown below. Journal subscriptions are sold on a per volume basis only. Claims for nonreceipt of issues will be honored if made within three months of publication of the issue. **See Publication Schedule Information.** Subscriptions are available for microform editions; details will be furnished upon request.

All issues are dispatched by airmail throughout the world.

Subscription Rates
available only to ind
the journal is for the
sent directly to the P

ie: ECU 67.00*. This price is
journal OR who warrant that
for mailing. Orders must be
personal check or credit card.

(Continued)

Separate rates apply to academic and corporate/government institutions. Postage and handling charges are extra.

*ECU (European Currency Unit) is the worldwide base list currency rate; payment can be made by draft drawn on ECU currency in the amount shown or in subscriber's local currency at the current conversion rate set by Publisher. Subscriber's should contact their agents or the Publisher. All prices are subject to change without notice.

Publication Schedule Information: To ensure your collection is up-to-date, please call the following numbers for information about the latest issue published: +44 (0) 118-956-0080 ext. 391; +1 973 643-7500 ext. 290; or web site: http://www.gbhap.com/reader.htm.
Note: If you have a rotary phone, please call our *Customer Service* at the numbers listed below.

Orders should be placed through one of the addresses below:

IPD Marketing Services,
PO Box 310
Queen's House, Don Road
St. Helier, Jersey
Channel Islands JE4 0TH
Telephone: +44 (0) 118-956-0080
Fax: +44 (0) 118-956-8211

PO Box 32160
Newark, NJ 07102, USA
Telephone: +1 800 545-8398
Fax: +1 973 643-7676

Kent Ridge, PO Box 1180
Singapore 911106
Republic of Singapore
Telephone: +65 741-6933
Fax: +65 741-6922

Yohan Western Publications Distribution Agency
3-14-9, Okubo, Shinjuku-ku
Tokyo 169, Japan
Telephone: +81 3 3208-0186
Fax: +81 3 3208-5308

Enquiries can also be sent by e-mail: <info@gbhap.com> and the world wide web: http://www.gbhap.com.

Rights and Permissions/Reprints of Individual Articles
Permission to reproduce and/or translate material contained in this journal must be obtained in writing from the Publisher.

This publication and each of the articles contained herein are protected by copyright. Except as allowed under national "fair use" laws, copying is not permitted by any means or for any purpose, such as for distribution to any third party (whether by sale, loan, gift, or otherwise); as agent (express or implied) of any third party; for purposes of advertising or promotion; or to create collective or derivative works. A photocopy license is available from the Publisher for institutional subscribers that need to make multiple copies of single articles for internal study or research purposes. Any unauthorized reproduction, transmission or storage may result in civil or criminal liability.

Copies of articles may be ordered through SCAN, the Publisher's own document delivery service. SCAN provides customers with the current contents and abstracts to all Gordon and Breach and Harwood Academic journals. Please contact one of the addresses listed above to receive SCAN, or view current contents and abstracts directly on the Web at http://www.gbhap.com, and for ordering.
The Publisher is also a member of Copyright Clearance Center.

This journal is sold CIF with title passing to the purchaser at the point of shipment in accordance with the laws of The Netherlands. All claims should be made to your agent or the Publisher.

SPANISH THEATRE 1920–1995

STRATEGIES IN PROTEST AND IMAGINATION (1)

Contemporary Theatre Review
1998, Vol. 7, Part 2, p. iii
Reprints available directly from the publisher
Photocopying permitted by license only

Contents

Acknowledgements

I would like to thank the Manchester Metropolitan University for granting me a leave of absence to put this volume together, and for funding the translation of José Antonio Sánchez and Mercè Saumell's articles and the interview with Lluís Pasqual. I am especially grateful for the support given by my Head of Department, Dr. Colin Buckley, and the Dean of the Faculty of Humanities and Social Studies, Dr. Stephen Kirby. Trudy Dunne, the departmental secretary provided administrative support and I am grateful for her willingness to undertake difficult typing jobs. Information Systems Management allowed access to their computing equipment and provided expert advice where necessary. For their encouragement and for many illuminating conversations relating to Spanish theatre I would also like to thank all the contributors, Olga Celda, Vicente Molina Foix and Maribel San Gines. Thanks are also due to my editor in chief at *Contemporary Theatre Review*, Franc Chamberlain, Antonio Gil de Carrasco of the Instituto Cervantes, Manchester, the British Academy, Sandra Hebron, Paul Heritage my colleagues in the department of English and History (especially Jacqueline Roy), and Henry Little. Special thanks must go to my graduate student, David Price-Uden who offered pertinent comments on the volume, editorial assistance and helped compile the index.

Contemporary Theatre Review
1998, Vol. 7, Part 2, pp. 1–5
Reprints available directly from the publisher
Photocopying permitted by license only

Editorial

Maria M. Delgado

This editorial seeks to introduce the articles contained in this volume, pointing to the areas of study included and the further topics in Spanish theatre studies which merit critical reassessments.

KEY WORDS: Spanish theatre, Spanish directors, Spanish playwrights, Spanish designers.

In 1995 the Union of Theatres of Europe based at the Odéon Théâtre de l'Europe chose to organize an exhibition at the Centre Georges Pompidou in Paris to celebrate the achievements of the Catalan director–designer, Fabià Puigserver, (1938–1991). It proved a high profile event demonstrating the influence exerted by Puigserver on contemporary stage design, an influence recognized by Brook in his comment that the history of set design is divided into before and after Puigserver produced the canvas membrane for Víctor García's *Yerma* (1971). The accompanying catalogue, containing a foreword by Giorgio Strehler, President of the Union of Theatres based at the Odéon in Paris, serves to situate Puigserver within a European framework, stating both his debt to a European tradition whilst drawing attention to his particular training in Poland and then Barcelona, and the specific context – time, space, text, director, cast, etc. – of each of his designs. An elusive subject uneasily situated within conflicting and intersecting landscapes, Puigserver's work (as both director and designer) and his writings demonstrate an awareness of the unstable nature of the theatrical text, and the many responses that can be generated from a single ephemeral stage moment. This exhibition has yet to receive a sentence of coverage in the British press. Just as his death went unreported – there was no obituary in any of the main newspapers or theatre journals (both academic and popular) – so have his achievements remained unsung. In a sense his fate is that of others whose contributions to Spanish theatre have largely gone unacknowledged. By redefining what constitutes Spanish theatre this volume seeks to accord visibility to areas too often ignored in the field of Hispanic theatre studies.

As such I have tried to commission articles on a range of subjects, rather than limit myself to the achievements of the playwrights of the period. All these articles are particular responses to Spanish theatre in the period 1920–1995. Spanish theatre is usually divided into pre- and post-1936, the outbreak of the country's traumatic and lengthy Civil War. This volume differs from standard practice beginning with a reassessment of the twenties and thirties looking at a period known mainly for the work of Federico García Lorca and Ramón del Valle-Inclán, its two most prominent playwrights. José A. Sánchez examines the stage practice (rather than the playwriting) of these figures and brings into his discussion an exploration of the work of Cipriano Rivas Cherif, probably the most important director of the time, and parallels with the radical experiments going on elsewhere in Europe. Valle-Inclán's achivements in anticipating the Theatre of the Absurd is dealt with by Robert Lima. Paul Julian Smith's article interrogates the re-sounding myth of Lorca, his evocation in films of the late seventies and eighties, and the treatment of his work in the hands of Lluís Pasqual. The role of theatre in the Civil War is covered by James McCarthy. He too attempts to view it within the political theatres of Europe – specifically that of the Weimar Republic and early Bolshevik Russia.

Martha T. Halsey and Phyllis Zatlin offer an assessment of Spanish drama after Lorca looking at playwriting during the Franco regime and its aftermath. Their informative article provides a commentary on the major protest playwrights of the Franco era – Antonio Buero Vallejo, Alfonso Sastre, and Lauro Olmo – and more controversial figures who have broken convincingly with the dominant dramaturgical structures, like Fernando Arrabal and Francisco Nieva. Their study concludes with a discussion of the current generation of playwrights including Fermín Cabal, José Luis Alonso de Santos and Sergi Belbel. A number of the figures mentioned by Halsey and Zatlin are covered in greater detail in other articles. Peter Podol's analysis of Fernando Arrabal's work exam-ines his often ignored Spanish roots and his promotion of an aesthetic of the grotesque which Podol views as deeply Hispanic. Gwynne Edwards focuses on Jaime Salom's position as a dramatist who has successfully moved from the constraints of working under the censorship prevalent during the dictatorship to enjoy a degree of critical and commercial success in the new Spain. The study of Salom pays special attention to his most adventurous play *Casi una diosa* (*Almost a Goddess*) (1993), a theatrical exploration of the relationship between Salvador Dalí, his wife Gala, and her first husband Paul Eluard. It has yet to receive an English language production – although it was given a rehearsed reading at the Traverse Theatre, Edinburgh in December 1993 – and a much acclaimed production at Madrid's Teatro Bellas Artes in February 1993. David George's study of the Catalan writer–director–translator Sergi Belbel does not deal principally with his work as a playwright, but rather concentrates on his directorial work, specifically his 1992 production of the turn-of-the-century Catalan dramatist, Àngel Guimerà's *La filla del mar* (*The Daughter of the Sea*) at Barcelona's Teatre Romea.

It is often forgotten, however, that Spanish theatre is more than just the history of a few playwrights. Major studies of Spanish theatre have paid scant attention to the work of directors, theorists, actors or designers. Francisco Ruiz Ramón's *Historia del teatro español. Siglo XX* (Madrid: Catedra, 1984), for example, although providing some information on the impact of the 'teatro independiente' is indicative of numerous other studies in its concentration on dramaturgy above all else. How welcome therefore to see La Asociación de Directores de Escena de España (The Association of Stage Directors of Spain) expanding the parameters of Spanish theatre studies by recently bringing out key studies of the work of José Luis Alonso, the prolific director who committed suicide in 1990 and the director–designer Fabià Puigserver who redefined Spanish stage design in the years following 1959 with his adventurous sense of colour, space and texture.[1] *El Público*, the influential theatre magazine published monthly by the Ministry of Culture, and tragically closed down after a dispute with the editor, Moises Pérez Coterillo, in 1992, provided key *cuadernos* (booklets) on figures and companies in contemporary theatre practice which included publications on Francisco Nieva, Cipriano Rivas Cherif and the Teatre Lliure. Nevertheless, for those who have no access to Spanish, these figures and institutions remain painfully distant. All however, receive some discussion in this volume. María Francisca Vilches de Frutos offers an informative analysis of Spanish directors who have hitherto received scant critical attention in English. John London provides an illustrated study of modern Spanish stage design. Stephen Roberts offers a reading of the Spanish philosopher José Ortega y Gasset's critical study, *Idea del teatro*, which posits some illuminating points about the function and purpose of theatre in twentieth-century Western society. My own article on the actor-manager Enrique Rambal provides the first English language introduction to a figure whose contribution to Spanish theatre in the period 1920–1956 has only recently been acknowledged to any significant degree. Mercè Saumell discusses the 'alternative' or Fringe theatre of the seventies and its continued impact. Looking beyond the established

---

[1] Juan Antonio Hormigón, ed., *Jose Luis Alonso: Teatro de cada día* (Madrid: Asociación de Directores de España, 1991) and G. J. Graells and J. A. Hormigón, eds., *Fabià Puigserver: Hombre de teatro* (Madrid: Asociación de Directores de España, 1993).

Catalonian groups like Els Joglars, Els Comediants and La Fura dels Baus, her article provides a thorough introduction to the performance groups which sprung up throughout Spain in the period. To conclude the volume, Lluís Pasqual, the former Artistic Director of the Centro Dramático Nacional, offers his own views on twentieth-century Spanish theatre. Engaging in discussion on a variety of topics relating to his own theatre practice he offers an alternative perspective on some of the topics discussed in other essays.

I do not pretend that this volume is exhaustive. There is a need for a reassessment of Jacinto Benavente's (1866–1954) achievements. The Nobel Prize-winning playwright has too often been viewed as the purveyor of trite comedies, but this fails to do justice to his eclectic output. There has been very little written on performance styles or actors who have made a significant contribution to twentieth-century Spanish theatre, and although Margarita Xirgu (1888–1969) Núria Espert (b.1935), and Josep Maria Flotats (b.1939), are mentioned in the Sánchez article and the Pasqual interview, all deserve major studies in their own right. Other figures not dealt with here in detail, like the underground playwrights of the Franco years, the avant-garde playwrights of the seventies such as Antonio Gala and Francisco Nieva, and the comedies of the Franco era, have already received critical attention in previous studies.[2]

One of the most exciting aspects of Spanish theatre in the past ten years have been the range of productions seen on the stages of Madrid and Barcelona. It is therefore unfortunate that the only productions to have reached Britain are the more stolid stagings of the Teatro Clasico which visited the Edinburgh Festival in 1989 and the Spanish Arts Festival in London in 1994. Key productions of Lorca and Valle-Inclán's work which played a crucial part in reawakening interest in these figures in the 1980s and 1990s, despite visiting France and Italy, never reached Britain. A Valle-Inclán renaissance initiated by Pasqual's 1984 landmark production of *Luces de bohemia* (*Bohemian Lights*) shows no sign of abating.[3] 1995 alone saw José Luis Gómez inaugurate his Teatro de la Abadia – a two space venue which will also provide a key centre for training in performance studies – with a sharp resonant production of

[2] See George Wellwarth, *Spanish Underground Drama* (University Park and London: The Pennsylvania State University Press, 1972), and Martha T. Halsey and Phyllis Zatlin, eds., *The Contemporary Spanish Theater: A Collection of Critical Essays* (Lantham: University Press of America, 1988). The recent *Contemporary Catalan Theatre: An Introduction*, edited by David George and John London (Sheffield: The Anglo-Catalan Society, 1996) is an excellent introduction to Catalan theatre.

[3] This is not to dismiss the influence of the first wave of Valle-Inclán productions in the 1970s initiated by Víctor García's *Yerma*.

Valle's *Retablo de la avaricia, la lujuria y la muerte* (*Savage Acts: Four Plays*). Barcelona's Teatre Joventut, a company who had failed to generate interest with their more recent productions, also scored a substantial critical success with their production of *La cabeza del dragón* (*The Dragon's Head*) directed by Alfons and Enric Flores. Visiting Barcelona in mid May 1995 – where Gómez's production was playing at El Mercat de les Flors – it was gratifying to see packed houses for plays which had hitherto enjoyed few major productions.

Although Valle may have failed to generate such substantial interest in Britain, this cannot be said of his friend and contemporary García Lorca. A deluge of Lorca productions hit Britain in the 1980s,[4] providing a phenomenon generally and perhaps unkindly regarded as 'Lorcaitus'. As Spain's status changed and she became part of the 'official' structures of Europe, there has been a renewed interest in her cultural wares. Lorca offered what appeared an easy point of contact with the country's more exotic customs and traits. A trail of folkloric productions reading the plays through easy clichés ensued. Although the trail looks certain to continue, I hope this volume will not only indicate the perils of such readings but also introduce to non-Spanish readers the range of material before and beyond Lorca that constitutes twentieth-century Spanish theatre.

Originally, the volume was conceived as a single publication and I have thus organized the contents chronologically rather than conceptually. This may explain what appears to be a rather strange grouping of articles that, for the purposes of publication, have been divided into three parts. As such those who wish to locate the material on dramaturgy, should consult in addition to the articles in Part 1 on the pre-Civil War theatre and Martha Halsey and Phyllis Zatlin's study of dramaturgy in the period post-1939, Podol's article on Arrabal in Part 2 and the following articles in Part 3: Gwynne Edwards' study of Salom and Post-Franco Spanish theatre, David George's essay on Belbel's production of Guimerà's *La filla del mar*, and Paul Julian Smith's examination of the use of Lorca in 1980s Spain. Articles on Spanish production history and theatrical theory make up the majority of Part 2, and open and close Part 3.

---

[4] See Gwynne Edwards, 'Lorca on the English Stage: Problems of Production and Translation', *New Theatre Quarterly*, 4, no. 16, November 1988, pp. 344–355, Maria M. Delgado and Gwynne Edwards, 'From Madrid to Stratford East: *The Public in Performance*', *Estreno*, 16, no. 2, Autumn 1990, pp. 11–18, and Maria M. Delgado, 'Marketing Lorca and Lawrence Till's *Blood Wedding*', *Estreno*, 21, no. 2, Autumn 1995, pp. 45–48.

Contemporary Theatre Review
1998, Vol. 7, Part 2, pp. 7–30
Reprints available directly from the publisher
Photocopying permitted by license only

'The Impossible Theatre': The Spanish Stage at the Time of the Avant-Garde*

José Antonio Sánchez (translated by Jill Pythian)

This article offers a general overview of the new Spanish theatre during the twenties and thirties. The first section covers the trends in scenic renovation promoted by Rivas Cherif, Valle-Inclán and García Lorca, among others, and reviews the main premieres, both in the professional and in the experimental and university fields. The second section attempts to synthesize the ideas derived from the texts of playwrights and critics which could form part of scenic models not applied in their time, attempting to show the parallels between these authors and avant-garde European theatre of the period.

KEY WORDS: Rivas Cherif, García Lorca, Spanish theatre, Avant-Garde theatre.

'Right now, generally speaking, [Spanish theatre] is theatre for pigs, by pigs. It's theatre made by pigs, aimed at pigs.' That was García Lorca's crushing response in 1933 when a journalist, after having interviewed him about La Barraca, wanted to know the poet's opinion on contemporary professional theatre in Spain.[1] Lorca's pronouncement is reminiscent of Artaud's famous remark about writers, though in the Spaniard's case the virulence and bitterness seem more justified. With similar scorn, Valle-Inclán had declared a few years previously that he had never written, nor would he ever write for Spanish actors,[2] and his theatrical creations were in fact kept much further away from the professional stages of Madrid than those of Lorca.

---

*Dedicated to Oscar Gómez, Juan Loriente, Carlos Marqueríe, Olga Mesa and Sara Molina, who continue committed to the truth and beauty of an impossible theatre.

[1] Francisco Pérez Herrero, 'Nuevo Carro de Tespis', La Mañana, Leon, August 1933. All translations from the Spanish undertaken by the translator.

[2] '... I have never written for Spanish actors, nor will I ever write for them ... Spanish actors do not even know how to speak. They stammer. And since none of them know how to speak, it seems stupid to write for them. That would be bringing myself down to the level of illiterates.' (ABC, 23 June 1927).

Spanish theatre from the first decades of this century is, in fact, characterized by a tragic imbalance between the plans for a renovation of the stage that were formulated by some dramatists, critics and intellectuals, and the outdated concept of the profession that was prevalent in most Spanish theatre companies at that time. This imbalance (paralleling that which existed between the intellectuals of the Republic and the masses which permitted the violent eruption of fascism) meant that most of the aforementioned ideas were only realized in amateur productions, or in a greatly compromised form in professional productions. In short, the concept of contemporary Spanish theatre implied by both, the dramatic and theoretical works of the writers mentioned above, and those of a few critics, intellectuals and theatre professionals, had little to do with the reality of a theatre that retained nineteenth-century methods of organization (companies that were built around a single actress or actor, to whose characteristics dramatists adapted their work, and that performed in theatres run by businessmen with more interest in economic matters than in art), and which appeased the lowest tastes of the bourgeois audience with post-Romantic melodramas like those of Echegaray, comic novelties or *costumbrista* works (Comedies of manners) like those of Carlos Arniches or the Álvarez Quintero Brothers, or at best, the elegant but empty 'well-made' plays of Benavente.

However, the landscape of Spanish stage creation, although desolate, did contain a few exceptions. Principal among these was Cipriano de Rivas Cherif, a friend of Valle-Inclán, with whom he collaborated on several theatrical productions. He played a central role in most of the attempts to renovate Spanish theatre during the twenties. At his instigation, Margarita Xirgu left the commercial repertory stage for good, and together they staged the first productions of works by Valle, Miguel de Unamuno, Rafael Alberti and Lorca. The latter, for his own part, and despite his general indictment of Spanish theatre, had allowed performances of his work, not only by Xirgu, but also by Gregorio Martínez Sierra and by Josefina de Artigas, and he actively collaborated with some semi-professional companies. There were also others who made more or less successful attempts at renovation, and although this never went as far as the dramatists had requested, it is necessary to reconstruct what was actually realized, before recounting what they had really wanted to do.

Attempts

Towards an Art Theatre

In 1923, during a dinner held by the PEN Club in Madrid, Rivas Cherif defended the idea of setting up in that city 'the idealistic, poetic, so-called "intimate" theatre, that exists in Barcelona under the direction of

Adrià Gual'. The Catalan dramatist and director had been running, since the last years of the nineteenth-century, a chamber theatre, which he himself called 'exceptional'. It was conceived as a laboratory in which to try out new theatrical forms on an extremely wide repertoire, which also included contemporary international plays. There were also experiments with a form of staging connected with the success of the modernist aesthetic in Catalonia.[3]

The first attempt at an art theatre in Madrid was made by Gregorio Martínez Sierra. Following on from the modernism of his first productions, Martínez Sierra decided in 1913 to set up a company with the name 'Teatro de Arte', which would attempt to apply the models of Max Reinhardt (whose work he knew and admired), Stanislavsky and Meyerhold, as well as the ideas of Edward Gordon Craig, Adolphe Appia and Fritz Erler. One of its most important features was the central role given to designers. Martínez Sierra frequently collaborated with Siegfried Burmann, Manuel Fontanals and Rafael Pérez Barradas. Burmann had been a disciple of Reinhardt, and after a period in Paris, he moved to Spain, where he proved highly influential.[4] Despite the eclecticism of his designs, he introduced new set design techniques to Spain, which differed from those of the traditional painted backcloths, and in the Teatro Eslava, home of the Teatro de Arte company, he managed to establish a set-building workshop, which allowed him to have direct control over the set-building process. The other great set designer, Fontanals, was trained as a draughtsman and furniture designer, and had never had any contact with the theatre until his meeting with Martínez Sierra. When the Teatro de Arte closed, Fontanals and Burmann became the most sought-after set designers in Madrid, and they created a certain style of set which, despite its disparity with what had gone before in terms of style and simplicity, still evoked the idea of a painted backcloth.

The importance of the set designers and Martínez Sierra's own interests ensured that the Teatro Eslava tended towards the spectacular. Some of its most famous productions were the premieres of ballets by Manuel de Falla: *El amor brujo* (*A Love Bewitched*) in 1915, with sets and costumes by the symbolist painter from the Canary Islands, Néstor, and *El sombrero de tres picos* (*The Three Cornered Hat*) in 1917 (two years before Serge Diaghilev's London production). As well as those two productions, mention should be made of the productions of Jacinto Grau's *El hijo pródigo* (*The Prodigal Son*) in 1918, and García Lorca's *El maleficio de la mariposa* (*The Butterfly's Evil Spell*) in 1920, with sets by Fernando

---

[3] Adrià Gual, 'Els petits cenacles', *La Revista*, September 1923, p. 159.
[4] Ana María Arias de Cossio, *Dos siglos de escenografía en Madrid* (Madrid: Monadori, 1991), p. 257.

Mignoni and costumes by Pérez Barradas, which resulted a commercial failure, and was only performed four times. However, these productions (like the Spanish productions of Ibsen's *A Doll's House* or Bernard Shaw's *Pygmalion*), were exceptions within the output of the Eslava, which was principally fed by writers such as Arniches, Pedro Muñoz Seca and Eduardo Marquina, generally satisfying the tastes of the mainstream audience that, in theory, ought to have shyed away from such an art theatre. Failure with the repertoire and the technical failings of the theatre provoked criticism from Rivas Cherif, who compared Diaghilev's production of de Falla's *El sombrero de tres picos* at the Opéra de Paris (with sets designed by Picasso) with the 'pantomime of performance' of the same work directed by Martínez Sierra, and did not hesitate to nickname the Teatro de Arte 'the Company That Wants To But Can't'.[5]

Cipriano Rivas Cherif (1891–1967) could be considered the first Spanish stage director in the modern sense of the word. A period in Italy between 1911 and 1914 allowed him to become acquainted with the work of Gordon Craig, who was to become his greatest inspiration and role model, and from whom he acquired many ideas, especially regarding lighting, stage architecture, the 'Supermarionette' theory and, in particular, the re-establishment of the stage director as the creator of a production. While in other European countries, the central role of the stage director had been taken for granted from around 1920, in Spain its appropriateness was still being questioned by such prestigious critics as Díez Canedo, afraid that the director's intervention would endanger the supreme importance of the text. Few shared Rivas Cherif's concept of a stage director as the author of a work differing from the written text,[6] so much so that even when the Spanish director fulfilled that role in Margarita Xirgu's company, he had to be credited as literary advisor, since the term 'stage director' had not yet been accepted into theatrical terminology.

During a stay in Paris in 1919–1920 (together with Manuel Azaña, future President of the Republic), Rivas Cherif discovered the work of Aurélien Lugné-Poe, Diaghilev, Georges Pitoëff, Firmin Gémier, and particularly Jacques Copeau, whom he considered to be 'the most original interpreter, in the French style, of the ideas of Gordon Craig'.[7] As soon as he returned to Spain, Rivas Cherif devoted himself fully to directing for the stage. In 1920, motivated socially as well as artistically, he staged Ibsen's *An Enemy of the People* at the Teatro de la

---

[5] Cipriano de Rivas Cherif, *Cómo hacer teatro* (Valencia: Pre-Textos, 1991), p. 273.
[6] *Idem.*, p. 253. Similar ideas are put forward by the critic Manuel Pedroso in the *Heraldo de Madrid*, 14 May 1924.
[7] Manuel Aznar, *Valle-Inclán, Rivas Cherif y la renovación teatral española (1907–1936)* (Barcelona: Cop d'Idees T.I.V., 1992), p. 21.

Escuela Nueva, taking popular Soviet theatre as his reference point.[8] In 1921, after a failed attempt to continue his work under the name of 'Teatro de los amigos de Valle-Inclán' ('Theatre of the Friends of Valle-Inclán'), Rivas Cherif staged a programme at the Madrid Ateneo, with works by Shakespeare, Synge and Cervantes, and announced forthcoming productions of Unamuno, Schnitzler and Valle-Inclán, although these never materialized for economic reasons.[9]

After two years as director of publicity at Vittorio Prodecca's Teatro dei Piccoli, and another two as adviser to Mimí Aguglia's company (who staged Valle-Inclán's *La cabeza del Bautista* [*The Head of the Baptist*] in 1924), Rivas Cherif undertook another venture into experimental theatre with the company El Mirlo Blanco, set up as a chamber theatre in the house of the Barojas. The venture received a lot of attention on the part of educated critics as the embryonic form of a new art theatre. Four different programmes were offered, each comprising two or three plays. The first one, produced on 6 February 1926, included the prologue and epilogue of Valle-Inclán's *Los cuernos de don Friolera* (*The Horns of Don Friolera*) together with other works by Ricardo and Pío Baroja, and on 8 March of the same year it included *Ligazón* (*Blood Pact*), a shadow play written by Valle especially for El Mirlo Blanco.

The opening of the new Círculo de Bellas Artes building allowed the chamber theatre to move to a larger space (although the stage dimensions still remained reduced). The company was renamed El Cántaro Roto, and it was joined by Valle-Inclán as project director. The inaugural programme consisted of a performance of *La Comedia Nueva o el café* (*The New Play or the Café*) by Moratín, followed by a new version of *Ligazón*, and in the second programme, the second play was replaced by Baroja's *Arlequín, mancebo de botica* (*Harlequin, Pharmacy Assistant*). The experiment was cut short at this point, partly due to economic problems, and partly due to Valle-Inclán's incorrigible impertinence in dealing with the authorities in charge of the Círculo de Bellas Artes.

After a period of deep depression, which rendered him inactive for several months, and a brief reappearance with El Mirlo Blanco, Rivas Cherif founded a new company, El Caracol, in 1928. This time he had his own venue: a rented basement in the Calle Mayor that was known as the Sala Rex. The theatre opened in November 1928 with a programme comprising *Lo invisible* (*That Which is Invisible*) by Azorín (who appeared in the production himself, reading the prologue), the short

---

[8] C. Rivas Cherif, 'Divagación a la luz de las candilejas', *La Pluma*, no. 3, August 1920, pp. 113–119.
[9] For more information regarding this or later productions by Rivas Cherif, consult the book compiled by Juan Aguilera and Manuel Aznar, *Cipriano de Rivas Cherif: retrato de una utopía* (Madrid: Centro de Documentation Teatral, 1989).

works *Doctor Death de 3 a 5* (*Doctor Death From 3 to 5*) and *La arañita en el espejo* (*The Little Spider in the Mirror*), again by Azorín, and Chekhov's *El oso* (*The Bear*), whose inclusion was intended as a homage to the Moscow Art Theatre.

The Sala Rex was where Rivas Cherif was able to get closest to his concept of a modern theatre, although spatial and economic restrictions continued to hamper the development of a form of staging in tune with his ideas. He did, however, make a clear display of the autonomy of stage creativity in relation to literary creativity when on December 6th, he staged *Despedida a Rubén* (*Farewell to Rubén*), a performance including poetry, music and dance. He declared that in his 'chapel' there was room not only for theatre, but for any communicative art form involving music and voice. This pioneering work was continued with the production of Jean Cocteau's *Orphée*, on December 19th of the same year, with sets by Salvador Bartolozzi and performances by Rivas Cherif himself in the role of Orpheus and Magda Donato as Eurydice. The company's final production was of a work by Rivas himself, *El sueño de la razón* (*The Sleep of Reason*). Its theme, lesbianism, alarmed the authorities of the Primo de Rivera dictatorship, who closed the theatre and confiscated the manuscript before the next work on the programme, García Lorca's *Amor de Don Perlimplín con Belisa en su jardín* (*The Love of Don Perlimplin with Belisa in His Garden*), could be performed.

Other initiatives followed during the first three decades of the century: the Teatro de Arte directed by Alejandro Miquis, with whom Gómez de la Serna collaborated, and who almost succeeded in staging his work *La utopía* (*The Utopia*); la Sociedad Nueva de Escritores Dramáticos y Líricos (the New Society of Lyric and Dramatic Writers); the Fantasio chamber theatre, at the home of Martínez Romarate, or the Teatro Cachiporra Andaluz, founded in Granada by García Lorca in collaboration with de Falla, in an attempt to rediscover the popular tradition of puppet shows.

As far as professional theatre of the twenties is concerned, attention should be drawn to two important productions. One was Ramón Gómez de la Serna's *Los medios seres* (*The Half Beings*), at Madrid's Teatro Alkázar, which the writer made into a kind of avant-garde soirée, despite the fact that neither the staging nor the text matched the radical nature of his intentions.[10] The other was García Lorca's *Mariana Pineda*, which was staged in 1927 by Margarita Xirgu's company, with the

---

[10] Rafael Flórez, 'Crónica de una batalla anunciada (el estreno de los medios seres)', in Angel García Pintado *et al.*, *La utopía de Ramón* (Madrid: Centro de Documencatión Teatral, 1988), pp. 20–21.

assistance of the writer himself, who collaborated with his friend Salvador Dalí on the set designs.[11]

Margarita Xirgu, although not involved in proposing the development of an art theatre, did make a decisive contribution in elevating the levels of artistry of the Spanish stage. Trained as a very young girl in working-class amateur dramatic groups, she gained some recognition for her role in Zola's *Theresa Raquin*, which gave her access to the professional theatre at the age of just sixteen. She played a wide variety of roles, collaborated at one point with Adrià Gual's Teatro Intimo, and ended up becoming, over very few years, the great actress of the Catalan theatre. Among her most important productions of this period, Oscar Wilde's *Salomé* and Hofmannsthal's *Elektra* especially stand out. Her acting technique was intuitive, although in her rare reflections on the subject, a connection can be discerned with certain basic ideas of Stanislavskian naturalism, even the method of physical actions. Those who attended her performances single out the expressiveness of her face, her soft but tense voice, and an enigmatic stage presence. As far as her work as a director is concerned, her main contribution was the maximum simplification of stage resources, and the construction of scenery based on real models taken from memory.[12] In 1915, she staged Valle-Inclán's *El yermo de las almas* (*The Wasteland of Souls*) in Barcelona, although even by that time she worked largely in Madrid, with Jacinto Benavente being one of the writers whose plays she regularly performed in. She established a repertory that combined contemporary writers (both from Spain and abroad), and classical writers, and in fact, it was in the field of renovating the staging of Spanish theatre of the Golden Age where Margarita Xirgu made one of her greatest contributions. Her meeting with Rivas Cherif, and the founding of the Teatro Español in 1930, marked the beginning of the most interesting stage of her career.

Towards a National Theatre

Just as attempts were made to create an art theatre in Spain, so critics and professionals during the time of the dictatorship talked of the need to found a national theatre based at the Teatro Español or the Teatro de la Princesa. During the time of the Republic, the discussions became formal plans, with the theatre's base moving to the Teatro María

---

[11] Of these, the critic Díez Canedo Writes: 'Designed with the eyes of a child, at once reminiscent of Picasso and school paintings of the most playful spontaneity, they are intimately interwined with the spirit of the play.' (Enrique Díez Canedo, *Artículos de crítica teatral. El teatro español de 1914–1936 V. Elementos de renovación* (Mexico: Joaquín Moitz, 1968), p. 134.

[12] Domènec Guansé, 'Toda una vida', in Enric Gallén *et al.*, *Margarita Xirgu, crónica de una pasión* (Madrid: Centro de Documentación Teatral, 1988), pp. 29–63.

Guerrero. The last of these plans was drawn up by Max Aub in 1936, and sent to Manuel Azaña. In it García Lorca, Rivas Cherif, Alejandro Casona and Martínez Sierra were proposed as directors, in a bid organized around the centrality and autonomy of the stage director, at the time that a need was becoming apparent for a new conservatory to train actors and directors, which was to be led by Rivas Cherif.[13] The fascist uprising of General Franco prevented the project from proceeding any further, despite its clearsightedness both in selecting the key players and in laying down the structure of such an organization.

In the absence of a National Theatre, the Teatro Español fulfilled that role. In 1930, coinciding with the establishment of the Second Republic, Margarita Xirgu's company, which had merged with that of Enrique Borrás, were awarded use of this theatre (from Madrid's Council), which lasted until 1935. Rivas Cherif collaborated with her as a literary and artistic advisor, although in actual fact he took on the role of stage director. Despite the nineteenth-century legacy within the company's organization, and the almost unchanging pictorial nature of the stage design, Rivas Cherif and Margarita Xirgu considerably raised production standards on the Spanish stage. They had the support of the major set designers of the time, Fontanals, Burmann and Bartolozzi, and they staged a very balanced repertoire, comprising works by writers such as Seneca, Lope, Tirso, Calderón, Goethe, Duque de Rivas, Hofmannsthal, Unamuno, Valle-Inclán, Benavente, Lénormand, Rice, Kaiser, García Lorca, Alberti, and Casona, amongst others. Following the models of Reinhardt and the Soviet theatre, Rivas Cherif organised open air performances in a wide variety of locations: most remarkable among these were the productions of Seneca's *Medea*, translated by Unamuno, and of Hofmannsthal's *Elektra*, both at the Roman theatre at Mérida, with no sets except the stones of the monument itself. Also notable were Calderón's *El alcalde de Zalamea* (*The Mayor of Zalamea*), which was performed in Madrid's Plaza Monumental, and Lope's *Fuenteovejuna*, in the town that gives the play its name.

In 1929, Valle-Inclán, who had not had any works produced for many years, allowed Irene López Heredia's company, for which Rivas Cherif had been advisor, to stage *El embrujado* (*The Bewitched*) and *Farsa y licencia de la reina castiza* (*Licentious Farce of the Throughbred Queen*), which he himself directed. In the same year, once the friction between Valle and Margarita Xirgu had been overcome, Rivas Cherif and Xirgu staged one of his great works, *Divinas palabras* (*Divine Words*). Surprisingly, this was a huge failure with audiences, a fact that Rivas Cherif bitterly regretted,

---

[13] M. Aznar, *Max Aub la vanguardia teatral* (*Escritos sobre teatro, 1928–1938*) (Valencia: Universidad de Valencia, 1993), pp. 135–151.

despite the defence of both the work and the staging made by critics and writers. The experience of this failure ultimately distanced Valle-Inclán from the stage, and resulted in him hardening his stance against the production of his plays, so far as to make him affirm that this was one of the worst tortures his sensibility had suffered: 'Everything is different to the way I intended it to be. Does the performance actually have anything to do with the stage directions I set down? I'm sure that my directions will give a more complete idea of what I had wanted to do than the performance does.'[14]

Another controversial production of that year was Rafael Alberti's *Fermín Galán*, a work about the Jaca revolt in the style of a *romance de ciego* (ballad of the blind), a failed attempt to introduce a strand of political theatre in Spain.[15] Critics, in general, praised Rivas Cherif's staging, Margarita Xirgu's performance, Burmann's sets ('admirable for the stylized simplicity of their design, and for the pleasing harmony of their colours'),[16] and the work of the whole cast of actors, something rather rare in a theatre still governed by the system of 'principal actors'.

The first work of García Lorca's to be performed at the Teatro Español was *La zapatera prodigiosa* (*The Prodigious Shoemaker's Wife*), in 1930. Lorca himself played the role of the Author in the prologue, and designed the sets and costumes, which were made by Salvador Bartolozzi. The critic Fernández Almagro emphasised the popular aspect that the sets and costumes provided 'with intentional childishness of execution and gaudy colours',[17] while Díez Canedo spoke of the 'rhythmic and mischievous charm, stylized grace and fine understanding of shading' displayed by Xirgu.[18]

Bodas de sangre was not given its first production by Xirgu but by Josefina de Artigas, with joint direction by Eduardo Marquina and Federico García Lorca. According to Francisco García Lorca's testimony, the poet personally directed the actors, who were used to a very different type of theatre: struggling against them, without them really approaching his objectives. Critics mentioned the difficult co-existence of literary values with emotiveness on stage, the relationship between the tones of the set and the dramatic emotion of the text, and the anti-realism of the stage discourse that showed 'an Andalusia that did not speak Andalusian'.[19]

---

[14] M. Aznar, *Valle-Inclán, Rivas Cherif y la renovación teatral española (1907–1936)*, p. 126.

[15] Alejo Carpentier, 'Teatro político, teatro popular, teatro viviente', in *Carteles*, 23 August 1931.

[16] E. Díez Canedo, *Artículos de crítica teatral. El teatro español de 1914–1936 V. Elementos de renovación*, p. 121.

[17] Fernández Almagro, *La voz*, 25 July 1930, p. 2.

[18] E. Díez Canedo, *Artículos de crítica teatral. El teatro español de 1914–1936 V. Elementos de renovación*, p. 136.

[19] María Francisca Vilches y Dru Dougherty, *Los estrenos teatrales de Federico García Lorca, (1920–1945)* (Madrid: Tabapress, 1992), p. 75.

The apotheosis of García Lorca as a dramatist came with the production of *Yerma* in 1934, this time once more under the direction of Rivas Cherif, in collaboration with Lorca himself, and designed by José Caballero and Manuel Fontanals. But this success only lasted a year. The staging in 1935 of *Doña Rosita la soltera o el lenguaje de las flores* (*Doña Rosita the Spinster or The Language of Flowers*) at the Teatro Español ended the writer's list of professional productions, since that of *La casa de Bernarda Alba* (*The House of Bernarda Alba*), planned for 1936 by the same company, was cancelled when the Civil War began.

Experimental Theatre and University Theatre

Despite working hard as a professional director, Rivas Cherif did not abandon his experimental and pedagogical interests. In 1930, he set up the Teatro Experimental de El Español, which opened with the premiere of *La zapatera prodigiosa* mentioned earlier, preceded by a medieval Chinese fable translated from the English by Rivas Cherif himself. The company's second production was *Un día de octubre* (*A Day in October*), by the German expressionist playwright Georg Kaiser, with sets designed by Burmann. But what interested Rivas Cherif most in the final years of the Republic were his plans for a theatre school, first in the form of the Estudio de Arte Dramático del Teatro Español (which in 1933 would become part of the Conservatorio de Música y Declamación, when Rivas Cherif joined that institution as a subdirector), and later under the name of Teatro Escuela de Arte (TEA), based at the Teatro María Guerrero. There he staged many experimental productions, with the collaboration of Felipe Lluch (stage director), Bartolozzi (set designer), and Enrique Casal (musical director).

One of García Lorca's most important contributions to Spanish stage directions is in connection with the Club Teatral Anfistora, established by Pura Ucelay. Between 1933 and 1936 he directed five works there, two of them his own: *La zapatera prodigiosa*, and *Amor de Don Perlimplín*. Although the first of these was practically a repeat of the production staged at El Español, the second enabled Lorca, despite human and material limitations, to put into practice a number of his innovative ideas, some of which are inherent in the initial text notation 'Teatro de aleluyas' (Theatre of Hallelullahs), which will be discussed below.[20] The set designer Fontanals collaborated on the subsequent productions of *Liliom* by Ferenc Molnár, Lope's *Peribáñez y el Comendador de Ocaña* (*Peribáñez and the Commander of Ocaña*), and García Gutiérrez's *El trovador* (*The Troubadour*); productions which gave the Club Anfistora the prestige of a real art theatre. The premiere of *Así que pasen cinco años* was

---

[20] F. García Lorca, *Amor de Don Perlimplín con Belisa en su jardín*, ed. Margarita Ucelay (Madrid: Catedra, 1990).

cancelled as a result of Lorca's assassination in Granada in July 1936, an event which also signalled the end of the club Anfistora.

Where university theatre is concerned, two important initiatives must be mentioned: the Teatro de las Misiones Pedagógicas, and La Barraca. Both had in common the aim of bringing the great classical Spanish repertoire closer to the lower social classes. But while the former was conceived as a travelling theatre, with the aim of bringing theatre to towns where it was unknown, the latter was designed to be a university theatre, based in Madrid, which could eventually tour around nearby Castilian towns. Alejandro Casona, as director of the Teatro de las Misiones Pedagógicas, strived to create a repertoire of simple plays, combined with dance and music, and performed with a minimum of props and/or scenery. Rafael Dieste, for his part, ran a puppet theatre variation, the Retablo de Fantoches or Guiñol de las Misiones, in which he collaborated with the painter Ramón Gaya. There were also other initiatives of this type, among them El Búho, Valencia's university theatre, with a similar agenda to that of La Barraca, and which became after 1936 a theatre of agitation and propaganda under the direction of Max Aub.

Within this field of university theatre, once again the most interesting contribution came from García Lorca. Although in the manifesto he spoke of the educative function of the classics and the social dimension of the scheme, Lorca did not renounce the introduction of renovating elements. That renovation began with the adaptation of the texts and the musical composition and arrangements: work often undertaken by Lorca himself. It continued in the rhythmic treatment of delivery, with special attention paid to silences and musicality, and it ended with the collaboration of excellent artists to design sets and costumes: Benjamín Palencia, José Caballero, Ramón Gaya, the sculptor Alberto, and Santiago Ontañón. Particularly interesting are Benjamín Palencia's sets and costumes for Calderón's *La vida es sueño* (*Life is a Dream*) (which incorporated an astrological backdrop and costumes that combined the popular and the surrealist); José Caballero's designs for *El burlador de Sevilla* (*The Trickster of Seville*) and *El caballero de Olmedo* (*The Knight of Olmedo*) (incorporating very simple elements at many levels), and those done by Alberto for *Fuenteovejuna* (based on backcloths painted with popular scenes).[21] One new element of renovation was the democratic organization of the company, freed from the system of principal and secondary casts,

---

[21] Reproductions of the designs and photographs of the sets can be found in Francisco Calvo, Ángel González and Francisco Javier Rocha, *La Barraca y su entorno teatral* (Madrid: Galería Multitud, 1975).

and which Lorca compared to a 'phalanstery'.[22] As a paid up member of the avant-garde, Lorca, who repeatedly declared himself apolitical, made his social preoccupation into an educational objective, and moved the political component from the theme into the plays' form and organization.

Models

Although some of the productions mentioned above were important, they did not completely embody the radical nature of their creators' stage ideas, and only made up a minimal percentage of the Spanish theatrical output during those decades. It would thus be misleading to argue that they were particularly effective in their objective of modernizing the theatre. The terrible consequences of the military uprising against the Republic affected the regeneration of the Spanish theatre in two ways: firstly, by preventing the continuation of stage productions by creators such as Rivas Cherif and Lorca, and secondly, by destroying the legacy of undeveloped ideas, both of those artists and of others such as Ortega, Pérez de Ayala, Valle-Inclán, Gómez de la Serna and Max Aub. The fact that this legacy has been reliant on written evidence and has mainly been the object of philological studies has for many years prevented a clear recovery of those ideas for the history of contemporary theatre. The following pages are a modest attempt to contribute to this task.[23]

The Anti-Realist Polemic and
The Reassertion of a Plastic Theatre

One of the starting points for the creation of avant-garde theatre in Spain has to do with the choice of an anti-realist aesthetic. Rivas Cherif claimed that the theatre should be rediscovered as 'an art of the imagination, and not merely an exemplary reproduction of the worst of everyday life'.[24] Similar opinions were expressed by Mauricio Bacarisse, Benjamín Jarnés and Díez Canedo: they stood in opposition to bourgeois comedy and mannered farces. In his 'Meditación sobre el marco', Ortega y Gasset saw the entrance to the stage as the opening to another world, 'the unreal, the phantasmagorical', and warned

---

[22] Interview with García Lorca by José María Salaverría, *La Vanguardia*, Barcelona, 1 December 1932, reproduced in *Idem.*, p. 24.

[23] In recent years, research has begun into Spanish theatre of the twenties and thirties; particularly notable are studies by Dru Dougherty, María Francisca Vilches, Manuel Aznar and Juan Aguilera.

[24] *Heraldo*, 7 August 1926, p. 4: cit. in Dru Dougherty, 'Talía convulsa: La crisis teatral de los años 20', p. 128.

against making the stage into a repetition of what the audience carried in their hearts and minds: 'it will only appear acceptable to us if it sends us gusts of fantasy, the air of legends'.[25] Undoubtably, Ortega's expectations would have been satisfied by a staging of Valle-Inclán's *Comedias bárbaras* (*Savage Plays*) which was conscious of facing the challenges of the unreal that the writer had posed: the sets of visions and shadows, the central dramatic role played by animals, the dream-like stage and the almost cinematic dynamism of sequences such as the flight of Sabelita down the night streets in *Aguila de blasón* (*The Emblematic Eagle*), all united under the myth-like tone that enveloped the stage presentation and the characters' actions.

The unreal is the point where works as diverse as those of Valle-Inclán, Unamuno and Azorín coincide. Unreality, in Unamuno's meta-physical theatre, becomes 'nakedness', a category that could be connected with the purification of the stage space proposed by Copeau, or earlier by Lugné-Poe,[26] and which gives Max Aub grounding to imagine a staging of Unamuno's *Sombras de sueño* (*Shadows of Dream*) in a theatre without a fourth wall, 'with no real set, surrounded by the audience on all sides: an island, isolated'.[27] More in harmony with Valle-Inclán's work, the novelist and critic Ramón Pérez de Ayala, after recognizing that naturalist theatre and analytic psychology could not last, predicted in his article 'Máscaras', a 'retheatricalization of the theatre'. During the years of the Republic only a few writers such as Ramón J. Sender and Max Aub defended, to a degree, the idea of realist theatre from a political perspective. But in general terms, the Spanish theatre of the avant-garde was much closer to this idea of 'retheatricalization', which should be associated with the models that arose from symbolism: Appia, Craig, Copeau, Tairov and Meyerhold.

Although Unamuno, Azorín and later Max Aub were unwilling to accept that the spoken word had lost its central role, the most lucid intellectuals and the greatest artists of the era understood that this principal of unreality had to be matched by a physicalization of the stage along the lines suggested by Craig. In contrast to the concept of theatre as the staging of a dramatic work, Ortega spoke of the stage as a place where painting, music and poetry would meet, giving the playwright the task of creating not a literary text but a 'programme of events', on the understanding that 'in an ordinary theatrical work, anything of real value can be fully appreciated through simply reading the play, with no

---

[25] José Ortega y Gasset, 'Meditación del marco' (April 1921) in *Obras completas II* (Madrid: Revista de Occidente, 1963), pp. 312–313.

[26] Ana María Arias de Cossío, *Dos siglos de escenografía en Madrid*, p. 247.

[27] Max Aub, 'Algunos aspectos del teatro español, de 1920 a 1930', *Revista Hispánica Moderna*, XXXI, 1935, p. 26.

need to go to a theatre'. As far as actors were concerned, Ortega demanded that they stop being merely interpreters of the written work, in order to become acrobats, dancers, mimes, jugglers, converting their plastic bodies into a universal metaphor. It is in fact precisely this physical reality that makes all the difference here. It is through physicalization that a magical transformation occurs, creating the 'phantasmagoria' conceived by the playwright.[28]

Ramón Gómez de la Serna was one of the first to champion the concept of a physical and visual theatre. During his stay in Paris in 1909–1910, he became fascinated by the popular stagings of pantomimes, and on his return to Spain the first dramatic work he published was itself a pantomime: *La bailarina* (*The Dancer*). His interest in the non-verbal dimension of theatre led him to play with images in the same way he played with words, and this is evident (despite the weakness of the work and its failure on opening) in the construction of *Los medios seres* (*The Half Beings*). This was apparent not only in the fact that the actors had half of their bodies and costumes painted black, in a visual interpretation of the characters' half-lives, but also in the attention given to stage colouring and to the dynamism of the stage composition. However, it is without doubt in a few shorter works that Gómez de la Serna's obsession with plasticity becomes more explicit: *La utopía* takes place in a shop that sells religious icons, with these becoming the protagonists on stage, and *El lunático* (*The Lunatic*) begins with an extremely long passage of stage directions, in which minute detail of an almost pictorial quality is used to describe the appearance of the protagonist's office and the characterization of the cast.[29]

The Cinematic Model

Gómez de la Serna's interest in visual performance was undoubtedly linked to the fascination felt in those years for silent movies. It gave grounding to the imagination in 'a kind of physical symphony ... a pure "ballet" of shapes and colours within a rhythm' (which is clearly associated with Gómez de la Serna's idea of pantomime), but the cinema was also considered by critics and artists alike to be the first step in the replacement of intellectual culture with a culture of the senses. While Antonio Espina emphasized the dynamism of the screen, Rivas Cherif focussed on the perspectivism that the cinema allowed,

---

[28] J. Ortega y Gasset, *Ideas sobre el teatro y la novela* (Madrid: Revista de Occidente/Alianza Editorial, 1982), pp. 70–95.
[29] Ignacio Soldevilla, 'Ramón Gómez de la Serna entre la tradición y la vanguardia', in Maria Francisca Vilches y Dru Dougherty, *El teatro en España entre la tradición y la vanguardia (1918–1939)*, pp. 69–78, p. 77.

as opposed to the static nature of the theatre, and Enrique Lafuente showed the possibilities of presenting the real and the imaginary simultaneously.[30] Faced with the narrative and spectacular possibilities of the cinema, some thought that the only way the theatre could survive was to return to pure drama. Others, with greater insight, accepted the challenge and tried to take what they could from the new developments, from the cinema's new rhythm and aesthetic.

On one occasion a journalist remarked to Valle-Inclán that he had been seen going to the cinema, and even to a Salon de Varietés (Music Hall) in the company of Rivas Cherif. To this the dramatist replied:

Well, of course... Why shouldn't I go? Of course I go to the cinema. It's the new theatre, it's modern. It's visual; it belongs more to the physical senses, but it is art. A new art form, the new physical art form. Living beauty. And one day, the cinema and the theatre will come together and make a complete whole, two theatres in a single theatre. And then people will be able to meet up and pass their time in the theatre.[31]

Elsewhere, Valle-Inclán drew a link between the construction of a new Spanish dramatic theatre and putting an end to actors corrupted by 'a drawing-room theatre'. This would allow a new theatre to develop which 'had no stories or single sets: following the example of current cinema, which, without words or sounds and fuelling itself only from the dynamism and variety of screen images has managed to become a worldwide success'.[32] And when a journalist commented, referring to the failure of *Divinas palabras*, 'What a shame the theatre does not have the resources that the cinema has for dealing with this kind of work', the playwright replied, 'Exactly. *Divinas palabras* looks like a film script.'[33]

The presence of cinema as a model for Valle-Inclán's theatrical ideas is visible in several areas. Firstly, it is present in the construction of the works themselves. In the first decades of the century, cinema was seen as a series of postcards or animated photographs: Valle-Inclán compared it to a series of historical tableaux, a kind of visual narrative, related to the popular *romance de ciego*. Valle-Inclán shared with the young Brecht a fascination for American cinema, popular ballads and Shakespeare's plays. Using *Hamlet* as an example, Valle-Inclán explained how it is not the dramatic situation that creates the scene, but the

[30] Dru Dougherty, 'Talía convulsa: La crisis teatral de los años 20', pp. 6–7.

[31] Federico Navas, *Las esfinges de Talía o Encuesta sobre la crisis del teatro* (Imprenta del Real Monasterio de El Escorial, 1928), reproduced in Dru Dougherty, ed., *Valle-Inclán y el cine* (Catalogue of the retrospective organized by Filmoteca Española) (Madrid: Ministerio de Cultura, 1986), p. 9.

[32] *Luz*, 23 November 1933, in *Idem.*, p. 9.

[33] *El Sol*, 25 March 1933, in *Idem.*, p. 9.

inverse of that: one begins with a spatial and visual concept to advance the dramatic action.[34]

Dynamism of action, continual transformation of the stage space, the introduction of the unreal into the real world: these facts connect Valle-Inclán's work with certain structural elements of expressionist drama. Such coinciding factors should have resulted in a similar treatment of stage space, and particularly of lighting. The interplay of light and shade, combined with voluminous sets, is where the key lies to staging Valle-Inclán's impossible theatre. His shadow plays provide a clue to the preference for a black and white aesthetic, another link with the cinematic model, and a factor discernible throughout his work.

The sensual dimension of Valle's theatre, however, is not restricted to his preoccupation with light: there is also an interest in the plastic, in the physical dimension, which goes back to his earliest written works. Speaking of the *Comedias bárbaras*, Rivas Cherif said that they appeared freshly painted rather than written, and that 'everything works on a visual plane', as much because of 'a certain outward manner taken from characteristic Shakespearian movement', as because of the Wagnerian musical tone in which his characters speak. 'Valle-Inclán is perhaps the only Spanish writer who frames his work with a pictorial atmosphere. He is surely to become a great stage director.'[35] Unfortunately, he never came to be one.

Puppet Epics

As an intellectual disciple of Gordon Craig, Rivas Cherif could not leave unexplored the possibility of linking Craig's stage utopias with the impossible plays of his friend Valle-Inclán, nor that of connecting the dream of a theatre without human performers with the dramatist's furious rejection of Spanish actors, whom he insulted on several occasions. However, the 'Supermarionette' theories of Gordon Craig were not interpreted by Rivas Cherif as a proposal for conventional actors, in the style of Meyerhold and the constructivists, but as a vindication of the puppet-show genre itself. Rivas linked this with the model of the *bululú* (a play performed by a single actor with the aid of puppets), and with the kind of production given by the Italian puppet company Teatro dei Piccoli, directed by Vittorio Prodecca. In fact, when the Italian's company, with which Rivas Cherif was to collaborate, played in Spain, Valle-Inclán

---

[34] Valle-Inclán, 'He hecho teatro tomando por maestro a Shakespeare', *ABC*, 23 June, 1927, reproduced in J.A. Hormigón, *Valle-Inclán. Cronología. Escritos dispersos. Epistolario* (Madrid: Fundación Banco Exterior, 1987), pp. 66–67.
[35] Manuel Aznar, *Valle-Inclán, Rivas Cherif y la renovación teatral española (1907–1936)*, p. 70 and p. 35.

announced, 'I now write theatre for puppets. I have invented something that I call *esperpentos*. This kind of theatre cannot be performed by actors, only by puppets, just like the Teatro dei Piccoli in Italy.'[36]

What most annoyed Valle-Inclán was the way actors spoke. According to him, they either screamed or stammered, with no middle ground. In the *bululú* he must have seen a means of more effectively controlling verbal interpretation. Rivas Cherif too, in his notes on acting technique, pays a lot of attention to declamation, particularly of verse, but very little to movement. Perhaps the impossibility of realizing this idea prevented them from imagining a play performed by actors using the physical and verbal discipline of puppets, something which Ortega did explicitly mention.

Apart from the confrontational and romantic implications arising from the use of marionettes in Valle-Inclán's theatre from the point of view of staging, the most obvious consequence is a distancing effect.[37] This effect is made explicit in the prologue to *Los cuernos de don Friolera*, when there is a juxtaposition of the way Shakespeare identifies with his characters with the superiority of the puppeteer over his puppets,[38] a distance which is evident to the audience. In this prologue, the character of Don Estrafalario, who is attending a *bululú* performance together with Don Manolito, complains about the antipathy and coldness of popular Spanish theatre, and reflects, 'If our theatre had the excitement of bullfighting, it would be magnificent.'[39] (It is also worth noting that Margarita Xirgu, a friend of Joselito, was fascinated by the spectacular nature of bullfights, and by how effectively they created physical, direct emotion, a fascination that led her to experiment with open-air theatre, in the Roman theatre at Mérida, Barcelona's Grec Theatre, in the Parque Retiro, and even in the Plaza de las Ventas.) But this theatre cannot be the result of a mere transposition of a popular genre to the stage (in the epilogue, Don Estrafalario asks Don Manolito to buy the *romance de ciego*, 'to burn it!'), but must instead be subjected to an artistic reconstruction, which Valle-Inclán calls a 'mathematic'. In the reference to the *esperpento* that appears in *Luces de bohemia*, the writer Max Estrella, after explaining that the real Spanish avant-garde is not that invented by the *ultraístas*, but that which follows on from Goya, notes that the 'tragic sense of Spanish life can only be expressed through a systematically deformed aesthetic', but that the 'deformation ceases to be one when it

---

[36] *Idem.*, p. 76.
[37] Jean-Marie Larvaud and Eliane Larvaud, 'Valle-Inclán y las marionetas entre la tradición y la vanguardia', in María Francisca Vilches y Dru Dougherty, *El teatro en España entre la tradición y la vanguardia (1918–1939)*, pp. 361–372 and p. 367.
[38] R. del Valle-Inclán, *Martes de carnaval (Esperpentos)* (Madrid: Espasa-Calpe, 1980), p. 76.
[39] *Idem.*, p. 75

is subjected to a perfect mathematic. My current aesthetic involves transforming classical norms through the mathematic of a concave mirror'.[40]

In this claim to be creating a new canon of deformed proportions, just as in the vindication of a sensual theatre in the face of the coldness of usual theatre, a certain harmony between Valle-Inclán and the general manifesto of historical avant-garde movements can be clearly detected. What is interesting, and makes all the difference, is that the invention of this new form suggested by Valle-Inclán, the *esperpento*, is the result of an interaction between a new expressive need and a popular genre. This is one of the keys to the renovation of Spanish theatre in the 1920s and 1930s: the absence of a sufficiently established urban bourgeoisie and of a tradition of bourgeois theatre developed during the nineteenth century (like that of Germany or France), meant that the alternative had to be sought within the popular. From this comes Valle-Inclán's orientation towards Galician traditions and the *bululú*, and García Lorca's towards puppet shows and Andalusian folklore.

The Poetic and The Popular

One of the most flawless of García Lorca's minor works, and one of the few he could direct himself, is *Amor de Don Perlimplín con Belisa en su jardín*, which is an 'aleluya', meaning it is taken from a popular story distributed on folded paper, where the narrative appears in the form of printed pictures with writing underneath, a genre very close, therefore, to that of the *bululú* and the *romance de ciego*. In the preliminary stage directions of one of the manuscripts, García Lorca describes green, yellow and white backgrounds, on which appear figures dressed in black 'with their hands and faces the colour of the background, and features drawn in black. The most absolute coldness and inexpressiveness are the main features of this kind of theatre'. Later he talks of 'austerity and inexpressiveness', and notes that the 'impression it should give is that it has been made geometrical, and is being told by a child from centuries ago'. The emotion it produces should be 'very distant, petrified', as if the life of the characters was 'connected to the rhythm of the world'. The characters are described as 'cold mathematical formulae', a formulae which the audience should be able to decipher to familiarize themselves with the characters' problems, since drama 'must be inside the audience but not inside the characters'.[41]

Although this treatment involves the elimination of the most direct element of emotion required by Valle-Inclán, it does maintain the idea

---

[40] R. del Valle-Inclán, *Luces de bohemia* (Madrid: Espasa-Calpe, 1994), pp. 162–163.
[41] F. García Lorca, *Amor de Don Perlimplín con Belisa en su jardín*, pp. 35–41.

of combining the popular with the artistic, and in a very similar form: a combination of the sensual with the mathematic and geometrical. Also noticeable in the stage directions is the suggestion of a theatrical aesthetic that has very clear links with expressionism and especially with the most abstract expressionism, or rather the theatre that is derived from it (Piscator and Brecht, on the one hand; Oskar Schlemmer on the other). What remains obvious is Lorca's interest in very simple staging, with a set design that is very stylized, almost abstract, and a strictly controlled use of gesture, using neither identification nor naturalism, but instead physical and musical action.

This insistence on the principles of mathematics and music is a constant in Lorca's work as a stage director. José Caballero, who collaborated with him on the design for the staging of *Yerma* in 1934, recalls the writer's desire that everything function 'with the same precision as clockwork, without a single mistake ... Because he wanted it to be a single poem read by several voices, without losing the rhythm and the inflections in any one of them, so that they form a controlled and matching whole'.[42] Lorca conceived the performance as a musical show, in which verbal interpretation and stage movement would be rhythmically integrated. 'It must be mathematic!'[43] was an oft-repeated phrase during the rehearsals for *Bodas de sangre* in 1934. Gerardo Diego, in his commentary of that play, enthused about the rhythmic nature of the resulting performance, and declared: 'Theatre is not, nor should it be, literature. It should be the spectacular meeting of Poetry with Sculpture and Music.'[44]

Also of particular interest is the way Lorca managed to translate the interaction of the poetic and the popular on a visual level into the set design. 'He had built up a picture', his brother Francisco describes, 'of the inside of a cave with entrances and lights at different levels. This sort of home is common in the province of Granada, where living in a cave is not necessarily a sign of poverty, since a certain geological configuration allows caves to be dug into the earth that are well lit and have wide interiors.'[45] In the same way that Lorca's lyric poetry is inspired by popular forms and subject matter, and his dramatic poetry springs (in the case of *Bodas de sangre*) from a real-life incident, his stage design was

---

[42] Alardo Prats, 'Los artistas en el ambiente de nuestro tiempo', *El Sol*, 15 December 1934, cit. in María Francisca Vilches y Dru Dougherty, *El teatro en España entre la tradición y la vanguardia (1918–1939)* (Madrid: CSIC, Fundación F. García Lorca, Tabapress, 1992), p. 244.
[43] Francisco García, *Lorca, Federico y su mundo* (Madrid: Alianza, 1980), p. 335.
[44] Gerardo Diego, 'El teatro musical de Federico García Lorca', *El Imparcial*, Madrid, 16 April 1933; cit. in Federico García Lorca, *Bodas de sangre*, eds. Allen Joseph and Juan Caballero (Madrid: Catedra, 1990), p. 38.
[45] Francisco García Lorca, *Federico y su mundo*, p. 336.

also inspired by a popular kind of housing, making it more simple and extracting all its rhythmic and formal potential, in order to obtain a result that corresponds to the idea of rhythmic space, articulated on various levels, almost abstract in nature.

The popular factor also manifests itself at another level in García Lorca's theatre: its social dimension. Following the model of Soviet theatre, Lorca, Rivas Cherif, and to a certain extent Xirgu, all aspired towards a theatre that combined renovation of form with the ability to communicate with the public. It was a matter of educating the audience without forcing their taste, and making theatre into accessible entertainment, either by establishing a standard ticket price at large theatres, or by taking theatre out to the people, and into open spaces.

The Theatre as Poetry Incarnate

However, together with his populist concerns, Lorca also maintained some strictly avant-garde ambitions in the field of staging, which are highlighted in the ideas visible in the 'impossible theatre' texts. Some studies have underlined the presence of expressionist elements in those texts, such as the abstract naming of characters, the existence of collective characters and symbolic characters, and the dramatic structuring into 'seasons'.[46] Other studies have suggested keys for the interpretation of Lorca's impossible theatre taken from surrealist poetry. But what is really required is an investigation of his thought processes at a largely stagebound level.

That which is known as Spanish surrealist theatre was linked with the strictly literary proposals made by writers such as Unamuno, Azorín, or Claudio de la Torre. In a way, some of García Lorca's 'Diálogos' accept this inheritance and make connections with the dramatic output of the French surrealists.[47] But García Lorca was aware that the renovation of the theatre could not come purely by means of poetic intervention: 'The problem of novelty in the theatre is to a great extent linked to the plastic. Half of the performance is dependent on rhythm, colour, set design.'[48] The stage play *El paseo de Buster Keaton (Buster Keaton's Walk)*, and the screenplay *Un viaje a la luna (A Journey to the Moon)* are two of Lorca's most fully realized attempts to approach this type of sensual

---

[46] Andrew A. Anderson, 'El público, Así que pasen cinco años, y El sueño de la vida: tres dramas expresionistas de García Lorca', in María Francisca Vilches y Dru Dougherty, *El teatro en España entre la tradición y la vanguardia (1918–1939)*, pp. 215–226.

[47] Perhaps the most radical of these are the 'Diálogo mudo de los cartujos' (a typographic translation of the characters' gestures) and 'Diálogo de los dos caracoles' (a series of images which could be related to the wordless dramas of Roger Vitrac). F. García Lorca, *Obras V*. ed. Miguel García Posada (Madrid: Akal, 1992), pp. 61–68.

[48] F. García Lorca, *Obras completas* (Madrid: Aguilar, 1964), p. 1774.

performance from poetic creation.[49] Both of these are clear examples of the use, in a surrealist form, of elements from the earliest American cinema, and while on this theme, it should be pointed out that due to his friendships with Dalí and Buñuel, it was in a visual, rather than literary sense, that Lorca came closest to surrealism.[50]

So even though the themes and images of works such as *Así que pasen cinco años* (*When Five Years Pass*) have an obviously surrealist influence, the same cannot be said of the formal structure and the mode of representation which that entails. The only effective renovation of the stage in Spain has been that introduced by Rivas Cherif, and Rivas' starting point was, like that of the expressionists, the ideas of Craig and Appia, the strengthening of gesture rather than psychology, of light rather than painting, of sound rather than words. The contribution of Valle-Inclán (and also that of Burmann) involved allowing the expressionist structures of staging also to be imposed on the impossible theatre of García Lorca, interacting with surrealist elements, and creating a mixture whose relationship to the theatre of Yvan Goll, though somewhat distant, could still be discerned.

While *Así que pasen cinco años* can be considered a performable drama according to the principles stated above, *Comedia sin título* (*Play Without a Title*) and *El público* (*The Public*) would have to be interpreted more as reflections on the nature and future of the theatre, written in a dramatic form, and not directly as dramas to be performed in a surrealist style (despite the excellent production that resulted from the interpretation of the second text by Lluís Pasqual in the mid-eighties). What García Lorca suggests in *El público* is the need to destroy the theatre in order to be able to express that which must be expressed. In 1929, at the time of writing this work, García Lorca wrote to his family from New York, 'We must think about the theatre of the future. Everything that exists in Spain today is dead. Either theatre must be changed, right down at root level, or it is finished forever. There is no other way.'[51]

This destructive impulse manifests itself in various places: in the rebellion against the repression of the mask/form, in the vindication of original dramas as opposed to the performance of stale tragedies, or in the director's final reflection:

---

[49] Julio Huélamo has brought together the common features of Lorca's dramatic works, particularly *El paseo de Buster Keaton* with those of the surrealists, in 'Lorca y los límites del teatro surrealista español', in María Francisca Vilches y Dru Dougherty, *El teatro en España entre la tradición y la vanguardia (1918–1939)*, pp. 207–214.

[50] Virginia Higginbotham, 'La iniciación de Lorca en el surrealismo', in *El surrealismo*, ed. Víctor García de la Concha (Madrid: Taurus, 1982), p. 244.

[51] 'Federico García Lorca escribe a su familia desde Nueva York y La Habana (1929–1930)', ed. Christopher Maurer, *Poesía*, Madrid, nos. 23 and 24, 1986, p. 78.

Breaking down all doors is the only way that drama can justify itself; seeing with one's own eyes that the law is a wall that dissolves in the smallest drop of blood. I am repulsed by the miserable man who draws a door on the wall with his finger, and then sleeps peacefully. Real drama is a three-ring circus where the air and the moon and the animals come and go with nowhere to rest.[52]

Lorca conceived his 'open-air theatre' as an exteriorization of his own internal world: the characters are no longer characters, they are not masks that have been given psychological individuality, but instead are poetic creations, that coincide with sensual creations on stage. The actor, meanwhile, should be able to physically transform the lyric content of the text, and interact with an abstract space, corresponding to that dramatic space which is free from the usual constraints of time and space, and is in a perpetual state of transformation, just as the characters themselves are.

Octavio Paz defines surrealism using three key terms: freedom, love and poetry. Dalí, on the other hand, talked of sexual instinct, awareness of death, and the physical concept of the enigma. These six keys are brought together in *El público*, but not only at the dramatic level, but also at a conceptual/staged level. The concept of the theatre as poetry incarnate ('the theatre is poetry that gets up from the book and becomes human') is linked to the idea of an interaction between the poetic/formal and the sensual/chaotic in the course of a theatrical performance. 'The theatre requires characters to appear on stage dressed in a suit of poetry, but at the same time with their bones and blood visible.'[53] The way to reach a balance between the mathematical principle of order and the liberation of instinct, love and matter on stage is the basic problem posed in *El público*: the tension that the director feels, aware that 'open-air theatre' can only be conceived as a limit, never as a reality, unless one chooses to actually live through theatre; in other words, to take the idea of a theatre of cruelty to its very limits. However, not even Artaud intended to eliminate the formal aspect of the performance: he too, like Lorca, dreamt of the possibility of creating a hieroglyphic score that would give form to the chaos of the passions. These must never be displayed openly, but should only remain allusions, like 'the outline of a hidden force'. And in this tension of the hidden, the theatre should live, but without ever renouncing that tension or the will to grow nearer to its manifestation.

Disturbing the audience, away from the comfortable lie of words, and making them confront the real problem, the problem of their own

---

[52] F. García Lorca, *El público*, ed. María Clementa Millán (Madrid: Catedra, 1988), pp. 158, 182, 184 and 185.
[53] F. García Lorca, *Obras completas*, p. 1810.

internal world, through the representation of the writer's internal world in a 'three-ring circus': that is the objective. Such a representation is impossible without recourse to the many properties of the poetic word itself. Through the remaining accounts of the rehearsals for *Así que pasen cinco años* in 1935, we know that Lorca devoted much attention to the sensual dimension of the performance: the actors were cast according to physical criteria, each character had to have a voice of their own, a way of moving, a personal rhythm, and Lorca was very attuned to small visual details. Unfortunately, the play never reached its first performance, which is why there is no visual record of the stage version of the only work from the impossible theatre that reached the rehearsal stage before Lorca's death. However, it is more than doubtful that it would have lived up to the radical nature of the ideas allowed by a reading of the text, and which Lorca never attempted to put into practice in an immediate form, as he admitted on several occasions. What García Lorca's surrealist theatre would have been like is something that, like the *Comedias bárbaras* or the *esperpentos* of Valle-Inclán, we can only imagine.

Conclusion

The enormous imbalance existing between the renovation of theatrical creation and the production mechanisms and tastes of the audience condemned the principal figures in the Spanish theatrical avant-grade to a life on the margins, or the renunciation of their most radical ideas. This imbalance caused both Valle-Inclán and García Lorca to seek an escape route through popular genres. This is the sort of theatre which, to some extent, and due to the intervention of Rivas Cherif and Margarita Xirgu, was actually performed. However, not even Xirgu could impose upon her company this new form of performance and staging which befitted works too advanced for the Spanish mainstream tradition. The situation would have been different if the plans drawn up in the Republican era had been followed through, particularly those for Rivas Cherif's Teatro Escuela, where a new generation of actors and directors would have been trained, and versed in the sensibility that would have fulfilled both the demands of the new Spanish writers and the stimuli received from the experimentation of the European stage. The triumph of fascism in Spain meant that the work of Rivas Cherif, Margarita Xirgu, García Lorca, Max Aub and others was cut brutally short. It would be necessary to wait until the late seventies and early eighties to see model performances of works by Lorca and Valle-Inclán. However, their most valuable legacy, the one that should enable the discovery of forms to fit our time, remains largely unrecovered. Those who wish to rebel, just as they did against the conservatism that reigns in current Spanish theatre, continue to suffer the same incomprehension and the same persecution as our greatest stage artists of the beginning of the century did during the hardest years of the Primo de Rivera dictatorship. The theatre still remains an intrinsically conservative art form, and now, more than ever, Lorca's dilemma is relevant: one must either destroy it, or learn to live within it.

Contemporary Theatre Review
1998, Vol. 7, Part 2, pp. 31–45
Reprints available directly from the publisher
Photocopying permitted by license only

Valle-Inclán, Spanish Precursor of the Absurdist Mode

Robert Lima

After an introductory section on his life in Spain and abroad, theatre background (acting, directing), and literary works (plays, stories, novels, poetry, aesthetics), pertinent plays by the Spanish writer Ramón del Valle-Inclán (1866–1936) are presented as evidence of the dramatist's precursory role in the evolution of the Theatre of the Absurd, a position now being recognized by critics and directors throughout Europe, the United States and Latin America.

KEY WORDS: Valle-Inclán, Ramón del/*Comedias bárbaras* (Savage Plays)/*Divinas palabras* (*Divine Words*)/*esperpento* / *Ligazón* (*Blood Pact*)/*Luces de bohemia* (*Bohemian Lights*)/Theatre of the Absurd.

It is too often the fate of an individual marked by genius not to be seen as such and, consequently, to suffer a lack of recognition in his lifetime due to the indifference, ignorance, or malice of his contemporaries. One such glaring case is that of the Spanish author Ramón del Valle-Inclán (1866–1936), one of the greatest writers ever produced by Spain. Demeaned by the cultural establishment of his own country, he was judged solely on his larger-than-life public persona and never accorded the status that he deserved as a cultural icon. He was better served abroad than in his own country.

Valle-Inclán was a man of many talents. The labels playwright, novelist, poet, aesthetician, and translator describe the writer of twenty-four plays, twelve novels, seven short-story collections, three books of poetry, two treatises on aesthetics, and five novels in translation. But this summation conveys only the literary aspect of Valle-Inclán's creativity. He was also a man-of-the-theatre, having been an actor, director and artistic consultant with a variety of theatrical companies, often on national and international tours with his wife, the actress Josefina Blanco, as well as a theoretician who expressed his ideas both vocally and in interviews. He worked as a journalist in his early career, had a stint as professor of Aesthetics in Madrid, was appointed to head several cultural offices in Spain and abroad, was a failed political candidate on several occasions, and served in honorary positions on various international writers' committees. He did all this despite a lifetime of serious illnesses, which required hospitalization and surgery on many occasions, and physical privation due to an income which kept him on the poverty level most of his years.

Ramón del Valle-Inclán was born on October 28, 1866 in Villanueva de Arosa, a coastal village in Galicia, the picturesque northwestern region of Spain whose roots are Celtic and Suevian. Educated in its environs, he went on to attend the university at Santiago de Compostela, still an important pilgrimage centre since its inception in the Middle Ages and zenith in the Renaissance. After abandoning his law studies in 1890 and moving to Madrid, he made a prolonged visit to Mexico, where he worked as a journalist. When he returned to Spain, he was a changed man. In Mexico, he had begun to develop a strong personality and in Galicia he dressed it in an outlandish garb. He was a mix of a belated romantic and an unkempt bohemian, his hair worn long under a large-brimmed hat, his eyes framed by large spectacles, his body covered by a cape or a serape. This early guise gave notice of his emerging theatricality, the public mask that he donned throughout his life to turn into public theatre his daily forays into street and café.

Such was the man-artist-mask that appeared in Madrid with his slim first book, *Femeninas* (Of Women) (1895),[1] which collected six short stories on love. An even smaller book, the novelette *Epitalamio* (Nuptial Song) (1897), followed it. But since sales of books by unknown authors did not produce much income, Valle-Inclán contracted to translate three novels by the Portuguese Eça de Queiroz and to adapt into a novel *La cara de Dios* (The Face of God) (1900), a play by his contemporary Carlos Arniches.

Joining other struggling writers in Madrid just before the turn of the century, he became an integral part of the group that would become known as 'The Generation of 1898', destined to become Spain's greatest community of creative writers and intellectuals since its Golden Age (1492–1680). Besides Valle-Inclán, the 'Generation' included the poet–dramatist Antonio Machado, the novelist–dramatist Pío Baroja, the essayist Ramiro de Maeztu, the novelist–essayist–dramatist José Martínez Ruiz ('Azorín'), the dramatist Jacinto Benavente (who would receive the Nobel Prize in 1922), and the philosopher–novelist–poet–

---

[1] The titles in English are in my translation and not italicized unless they have been published.

dramatist Miguel de Unamuno, among those who would become writers of international renown. Together they diagnosed the national malaise of Spain as *abulia*, the lack of will to act, seeing it as a product of 'living in the past' rather than looking to the future. 'The problem of Spain', as they termed it, culminated in the nation's defeat by the United States in 1898 with the consequent loss of its remaining colonies in America and the Far East. Due to their ongoing protests against all that stood for the 'old ways' that had prostrated Spain, the otherwise highly individualistic writers were christened 'The Generation of 1898' by one of their own, 'Azorín'.

At the time, seeking to concentrate on his art, Valle-Inclán did not write in newspapers and magazines about 'the problem of Spain' as did his companions,[2] but his actions on the streets of Madrid evidenced his sympathy with the Cuban rebels, as when he confronted a group shouting anti-US slogans and charged at them with cane in hand berating them as cowards for not being at the front. Such incidents led to his declaration: 'The Cuban War was won by the Cubans on their soil and by me on the streets of Madrid'.[3] Not only was he a man-of-action in such settings but he was especially notorious for his verbal tirades against the government, its functionaries, and the age-old policies that had led to the national disaster.

It was in his daily *tertulias*, gatherings in various cafes or other venues in Madrid, that he held sway. On those intimate stages he promoted a public image as an irascible individualist through bombast and a razor wit. It was typical of his generation of writers to possess strong, expressive personalities but Valle-Inclán outdid them all, both in voice and in figure. Still, his pronouncements were as often aesthetic as political. He could not tolerate the likes of the popular dramatist José Echegaray, who won Spain's first Nobel Prize in 1904, and he berated him and his ilk publicly whenever the occasion arose, be it among his cronies in the café or while in attendance at a play he felt was bad. On several occasions he was brought before the magistrate to account for his outrageous actions, especially in disrupting performances with verbal attacks on the play and its author.

And yet, despite what many of his unwitting contemporaries took to be mere superficiality in his words and actions, he came to influence a whole generation of writers and painters, both Spanish and foreign,

---

[2] For their statements, see my article, 'Crisis and Response: The Dynamics of Spain's 'Generation of 1898', in *Los hallazgos de la lectura. Estudio dedicado a Miguel Enguídanos*, eds. John Crispin, Enrique Pupo-Walker, Luis Lorenzo-Rivero (Madrid: Ediciones José Porrúa Turanzas, 1989), pp. 107–119.

[3] Cited in Francisco Madrid, *La vida altiva de Valle-Inclán* (Buenos Aires: Poseidón, 1943), p. 54. The translation is mine.

among them Federico García Lorca and Pablo Picasso, through insights into the creative process which he communicated in the cafes of Madrid and elsewhere. It has been said that if a Boswell had jotted down his pronouncements his stature as an innovative thinker would have been greater than that which his writings have brought him. Fortunately, many of his ideas on Beauty and the path to personal fulfillment – as man and artist – were brought together when he published in 1916 *La lámpara maravillosa (The Lamp of Marvels)*,[4] in which he explicated his evolution as mystic, aesthetician and writer. It is one of the singular documents of its kind in Spanish literature.

Valle-Inclán's initial period as a dramatist and man-of-the-theatre was very brief. It began in 1898 when he made his debut in Benavente's *La comida de las fieras* (The Banquet of the Beasts) in the satirical role of Teófilo Everit styled after him. Early in 1899 he performed again, this time in an adaptation of an Alphonse Daudet novel. His own first play, *Cenizas* (Ashes), was produced and published by Benavente in 1899, to help raise funds for an artificial limb; Valle-Inclán had lost his left arm to gangrene after a cufflink became embedded in his wrist during a café dispute. When he publicly forgave Manuel Bueno, the journalist who had inflicted the wound, Valle-Inclán's magnanimity made him a subject for Ripley's 'Believe it or Not'. The incident put an end to his aspirations as a professional actor, although not to his penchant for the dramatic action in public places. He also gave up the writing of plays when *Cenizas* met with an indifferent press.

He turned to prose instead writing exquisitely in the mode of Hispanic *Modernismo* but also demonstrating a prowess with dialogue, bred in the theatre, which remained in his blood even when he stepped away from the drama as a form of expression. The four novels collectively titled *Sonatas, Memorias del Marqués de Bradomín* (Memoirs of the Marquis of Bradomín),[5] which appeared between 1902 and 1905, brought his first popular success and literary notoriety due to the erotic nature of the works. The protagonist of these novels is a memoirist of his bittersweet love life; Valle-Inclán describes him as 'uncomely, catholic and sentimental', qualities which make him a unique modern variant of the classic Don Juan.

---

[4] Ramón del Valle-Inclán, *La lámpara maravillosa. Ejercicios espirituales* (Madrid: Sociedad General Española de Librería – Imprenta Helénica, 1916). See also the translation into English: *The Lamp of Marvels* translated by Robert Lima (West Stockbridge: Lindisfarne Press, 1986).

[5] English translation: *The Pleasant Memoirs of the Marquis de Bradomín*, translated by May Heywood Broun and Thomas Walsh (New York: Harcourt, Brace, 1924) and (London: Constable, 1925).

Since publishing was his only source of income, he devoted himself to writing with great tenacity and rapidly became a prolific author of long and short narratives, often selling the pieces to newspapers and serial publications. Among other books of this period were several collections of stories, most notably *Jardín umbrío* (The Shaded Garden) (1903), and *Flor de santidad* (Flower of Sanctity) (1904), a novel of pastoral life full of the religious credulity and superstition typical of Galicia.

Curiously, he returned to drama in 1903 through *Jardín umbrío*, including in the short-story collection a dialogue piece titled 'Tragedia de ensueño' ('Dream Tragedy'), and a second dramatic vignette 'Comedia de ensueño' ('Dream Comedy') in a later edition. These works were followed by the full-length plays *El Marqués de Bradomín* (The Marquis of Bradomín) (1907) which dramatized parts of his *Sonatas*, *Aguila de blasón* (The Emblazoned Eagle) (1907) and *Romance de lobos* (Wolf Ballad) (1908), the latter two belonging to the trilogy known as the *Comedias bárbaras* (Savage Plays), *El yermo de las almas* (The Barrenness of Souls, a revision of *Cenizas*) (1908), *Voces de gesta* (Epic Voices) (1911), *La marquesa Rosalinda* (The Marquise Rosalinda) (1913) and *El embrujado* (The Bewitched) (1913), which triggered a celebrated confrontation with Benito Pérez Galdós when the national theatre company headed by this prominent literary figure refused to produce the work. The second period of Valle-Inclán's involvement with the theatre ended because of this incident. Once again, he was a dramatist without an outlet for his work.

Even as he fashioned his plays, he continued to write other works. *Aromas de leyenda* (The Fragrance of Legend) (1907) was the first of his three books of poetry, the other two being *La pipa de kif* (The Pipe of Kiff) (1919) and *El pasajero* (The Passerby) (1920); all three were collected in 1930 as *Claves líricas* (Lyrical Keys). Among his novels were the three historical narratives of *La guerra carlista* (The Carlist War) (1908–1909). Much later came the masterwork which featured an innovative mix of Spanish American language, motifs and history, *Tirano Banderas* (The Tyrant Banderas) (1926), which won critical acclaim throughout the Hispanic world and was translated into English as *The Tyrant*.[6] Lastly, he published *La corte de los milagros* (The Court of Miracles) (1927) and *¡¡Viva mi dueño!* (Long Live My Master!) (1928), two in the ambitious series of novels collectively titled *El ruedo ibérico* (The Iberian Cycle), projected to portray nineteenth-century Spain but left unfinished at his death. In many of these literary works, which are replete with savagely satirical assessments of the nation's dilemma, he was belatedly expressing

---

[6] *The Tyrant. A Novel of Warm Lands*, translated by Margarita Pavitt (New York: Henry Holt & Co., 1929).

in writing the views that he had promoted earlier on the streets and in the cafes of the Spanish capital.

Knowing that he was seriously ill, he left Rome, where he was serving as a cultural ambassador of the Republic of Spain, and returned to his native region of Galicia for treatment. He had in effect undertaken what would be a final pilgrimage to the holy city, Santiago de Compostela. It was there that he died on January 5, 1936. Among the international tributes were special issues of many publications and the premiere performances of some of his plays. Federico García Lorca, who would himself die that year under tragic circumstances, joined Rafael Alberti, Luis Cernuda and others of the 'Generation of 1927' at Madrid's Ateneo in appreciation of Valle-Inclán's genius, the man having taught them so much in theory and in practice during their apprenticeship in the Spanish capital. It is ironic that García Lorca's death later in 1936 at the start of the Spanish Civil War, propagandized by the Republic and Communist sympathizers as the execution of a martyr to their political cause, brought him posthumous fame throughout the world while Valle-Inclán's death at the beginning of the same year in non-political circumstances had only normal repercussions. To this day Lorca's name is widely known (if not always for the right reasons), while that of Valle-Inclán, his sometime mentor, remains more obscure in the world theatre community. And this despite the importance of Valle-Inclán's work as an innovative dramatist and aesthetician.

Among the most masterly of Valle-Inclán's plays are the powerful social statements collectively titled *Comedias bárbaras* (Savage Plays). The internal chronology of the trilogy begins with *Cara de Plata* (*Silver Face*) (1922), the last published, continues with *Aguila de blasón*, and culminates in *Romance de lobos*, telling the story of the final years of anachronistic feudalism in Galicia, Valle-Inclán's home region. With Don Juan Manuel Montenegro at the apex of the anachronistic feudal order, the antagonism of sons and peasants scales the heights to tumble the protagonist from his perch. After the fall, there is a recognition scene in which Don Juan Manuel takes up the cause of the masses and leads beggar and peasant against his rapacious sons. But before he can wear the laurel of saviour of the masses, he is killed. The savage ways of father and sons have led to patricide. Although the term *esperpento* had yet to be coined by him at the time of their writing, Valle-Inclán's first-written *Comedias bárbaras* are, in effect, the earliest treatments in his drama under that aesthetic rubric; furthermore, they document an interest in such social causes as the plight of beggars, tenant farmers, and of others in the lower echelon who did not have access to a better life due to traditional class barriers and the manipulations of self-serving institutions, including the Church. Such concerns would become fully manifest in the *esperpentos* of the 1920s.

Over the long period of his career as a writer, Valle-Inclán's most important and lasting contribution was the aesthetic premise of the *esperpento*, which had been fully formulated by 1920, the beginning of the third and final phase (1920–1936) of his activity as a playwright and man-of-the-theatre. The basic tenets of the new aesthetic were posited through the words of Max Estrella, the protagonist of *Luces de bohemia* (*Bohemian Lights*) (1920), the first of the genre:

Our tragedy is not tragedy ... (It is) The *esperpento* ... Goya was the inventor of *esperpentism*. Classical heroes have taken a stroll along Gato Alley ... Classical heroes reflected in those concave mirrors manifest the *esperpento*. The tragic sense of Spanish life can only be rendered through an aesthetic that is systematically deformed ... Spain is a grotesque deformation of European civilization ... In a concave mirror, the most beautiful images are absurd ... Deformity ceases to be that when it is subject to a perfect mathematical system. My present aesthetic is to transform classical norms through the mathematics of the concave mirror ... Let us deform expression in the same mirror that deforms our faces, and the whole miserable life of Spain.[7]

The Callejón de Alvaro Gato in Madrid's old quarter, between Puerta del Sol and Plaza Santa Ana, still has the fun-house mirrors that distorted the images of passersby in Valle-Inclán's day. But while those street mirrors have lost much of their reflective properties over the years, the brilliance of Valle-Inclán's figurative concave mirrors has increased as his *esperpentos* are more widely read and performed.

Similar conceptions of the absurdity and deformity of society in his time prompted both earlier and later assessments akin to those formulated in *Luces de bohemia*. The poet had expressed himself in 1919 in *La pipa de kif*, a collection which showed the marked shift in aesthetics away from his initial *Modernismo* that would be paralleled and enhanced in his subsequent drama, while the critic promoted his ideas on the new perspective in interviews throughout this final period of his career in the theatre. In one, he stated:

There are three ways of seeing the world artistically or aesthetically: from the knees, standing, or from the air. When one adopts the kneeling position – and that's the oldest stance in literature – the characters, the heroes, are given a condition superior to that of human beings or, at least, to that of the narrator or poet ... There is a second way, which is to consider fictional protagonists as if they were of our own nature, as if they were our brothers, as if they were us ... And there is a third way, which is to see the world from a superior plane and to consider the characters of the plot as being inferior to the author, with a touch of irony. The gods become characters in a skit. This is a very Spanish manner, the manner of a demiurge who cannot conceive of himself as made of the same stuff as his figurines. This is the manner of Quevedo ... This manner is made definitive in Goya. And

[7] Ramón del Valle-Inclán, *Luces de bohemia* (Madrid: Espasa-Calpe, 1968), pp. 105–107. The translation is mine.

it was this consideration that moved me to take a new course in my literature and write the *esperpentos*, the literary genre that I baptize with the name of *esperpento*.[8]

Elsewhere, the author springs from purely artistic considerations to such socio-political concerns as the succession of inept governments that could neither better the miserable state of the peasant in the countryside and the worker in the city, nor rectify the many inequities of daily life in a nation that had not learned the hard lessons of 1898 when Spain lost the remnants of its once-vast empire through incompetence and an unrealistic belief in the viability of past glories. It was such concerns that formed the rationale for the new aesthetic of the grotesque and the absurd:

Ours is a harsh paternity ... Because we are ever accompanied by indignation at what we see taking place around us fatally. Spain is a vast stage selected by tragedy. There's always a dramatic moment in Spain; a drama well beyond the capabilities of the participants ... Our entire populace is seen to be worth less than a gang of trivial players set on staging the genial drama of Spanish life. The result, of course, is an *esperpento*.[9]

As Valle-Inclán had stated earlier, aberrations of social, political and religious traditions had been experienced and depicted in their respective eras by Francisco de Quevedo (1580–1645) and Francisco Goya (1746–1828). Theirs, too, were times of rapacity and inequities, each with its own peculiarities. Quevedo's sardonic view of life in Spain at the height of its power can be seen in *Historia de la vida del buscón llamado don Pablos* (The Life of Pablos the Rogue) (1626) and *Sueños y discursos de verdades descubridoras de abusos, vicios, y engaños en todos los oficios y estados*, collectively known as *Sueños* (Dreams) (1606).[10] Goya's embittered vision of Spanish society-at-large was depicted in such collections of etchings as *Los caprichos* (Caprices) (1797) and *Los desastres de la guerra* (The Disasters of War) (pre-1820), along with paintings of other grotesque subjects, most notably those referred to as the 'Black Paintings' in La Quinta del Sordo (The Villa of the Deaf Man); together they provided unequivocal evidence of the long and continuous history of the nation's social, political and religious

---

[8] Interview with the playwright Gregorio Martínez Sierra, 'Hablando con Valle-Inclán. De él y de su obra', *ABC* (Madrid), 7 December 1928, p. 1. The translation is mine.

[9] Francisco Madrid, *La vida altiva de Valle-Inclán* (Buenos Aires: Poseidón, 1943). The translation is mine.

[10] The five dreams or visions were written over a period of years: *El sueño del juicio final* (Dream of the Last Judgement) (1606), *El alguacil endemoniado* (The Bewitched Constable) (1607), *El sueño del infierno*, also known as *Las zahurdas de Plutón* (The Dream of Hell/The Pigsties of Pluto) (1608), *El mundo por dentro* (The World from Within) (1612), and *El sueño de la muerte* (The Dream of Death) (1621–1622). Sometimes editions have included an additional piece: *La hora de todos y la fortuna con seso* (Everyone's Time and Fortune with Brains) (1635).

grotesqueness. The condition was akin in its manifestations to what Henry James had termed 'the high brutality of good intentions'.

A similar attention to social incongruity, deformity and absurdity are present in all of Valle-Inclán's *esperpentos*. As with Quevedo and Goya, his concern was to depict the inhumanity of people toward one another, whatever the ambient, whatever the period. Often, as in the works of Quevedo and Goya, that inhumanity has a savage aspect. *Luces de bohemia* is at the beginning of a cycle of plays that study the variety of social savagery in Spain but which are, in point of fact, universal in their assessment of the human condition.

Luces de bohemia takes as its central concern the suffering and death of the protagonist at the hands of society. That suffering and that death are as chargeable to the people with whom Máximo Estrella comes in contact as if they had actually executed him with their own hands. Both middle and lower classes here are guilty of savage indifference to his plight as artist and man; it is that lack of recognition of his writings and the cutting off of his meagre source of income that lead to Max's unconquerable despair, thus making his death as inevitable as the fate decreed for the protagonists of Greek tragedy.

Further, even those who express concern for Max's situation cannot be trusted. For one, his avowed friend Don Latino takes the lottery ticket from a drunken Max and pockets the winnings after his death, never even thinking of sharing the money with the writer's destitute widow and daughter. In the depths of despair, the two women commit the act of suicide which they and Max had discussed early in the play. Frequently, the inhumanity of man to man manifests itself in tacit but no less savage ways than direct aggression.

The impact of this *esperpento* is even greater when its basis in the life of Alejandro Sawa is recognized. A flamboyant bohemian writer, Sawa had died in 1909 under conditions not unlike those described by Valle-Inclán in *Luces de bohemia*. The savagery of what was perceived as fictional in the play is revealed as a cornerstone of the reality of Alejandro Sawa's life as a novelist cruelly ignored by the establishment and his agonizing death as a result of the syphilis he had contracted, which had first blinded him. In portraying Sawa through Max Estrella, Valle-Inclán made his bitterest dramatic statement on the savagery of society, in this case directed towards the artist. In other *esperpentos* he attacked different segments of society and the culture that has given rise to its long-established institutions and hallowed traditions.

Divinas palabras (*Divine Words*) demonstrates yet other levels of savagery in a rural context. First, Lucero's verbal and physical abusiveness of Poca Pena, his mate, is seen in the opening moments of the play. Then, two deaths mark the indifference of society: that of Juana la Reina, is mourned ritually rather than emotionally by family and friends, while that of her idiot son Laureano goes unmourned. Indeed, the first death is seen as beneficial to the living relatives, who fight for possession of the trophy, the hydrocephalic dwarf; the second death is seen as oppressive in that the income produced from displaying the idiot's genitals disappears with his demise. The social savagery is pointedly underscored by pigs eating Laureano's cadaver. Yet another instance is Pedro Gailo's attempt to seduce his daughter, who fights off his drunken savagery and deftly avoids the incestuous liaison.

In the same pattern of sanctimoniousness and amorality, townspeople are about to stone to death the naked Mari Gaila for fornication, only to be halted by her foolish husband's last-minute mouthing of those words of Christ that had saved the Gospel prostitute: 'Let him who is without sin cast the first stone.' Recovering from the momentary hesitation, everyone again stands ready to throw stones at the prostrate woman until, astutely, Pedro Gailo utters the same words in Latin. Only upon hearing the Church's language, whose meaning has been lost to them and thus attained an aura of magic, is the savagery of the populace quelled. The words uttered in Latin have become the Divine Words of the title. Thus, it has taken a near-miracle to subdue the savage beast of a mob bent on mayhem and murder in the name of Christian morality. After the ritual with bell (ringing from the steeple), book (from which the Gospel words are read), and candle (held by Pedro Gailo) which has saved her from the imminent stoning, Mari-Gaila is raised from her crouching position and is led through the cemetery into the church by her husband in a symbolic rite of passage from death to rebirth. The savagery in her has also been diluted.

Ligazón (Blood Pact), a one-act play, presents a small social grouping, also in a rural setting. The work shows the savagery inherent in a context ostensibly Christian; it demonstrates the pagan substratum that lies close to the surface veneer of Spanish Catholicism. Elements of pre-Christian paganism come to the fore when normal means cannot provide the desired result in society. Thus, the three women in the play, two old and one young, speak with relish of the Black Arts which they practice with apparent success in their Galician village. And it is a profane pagan ritual instigated by The Lass that binds her's and The Knife Grinder's lust in a savage blood pact. But that act is only initiatory; the confirmation of their bond comes later, with their complicity in the brutal murder which closes the play so savagely. That dark deed makes the intimate blood pact transcend its personal consequences. A human victim has been sacrificed and the lifeless hulk given to the earth, which receives the body fluids passively, as if accepting a libation in an ancient rite of propitiation. The climactic blood pact has escalated the relationship between The Lass and The Knife Grinder to a savage complicity which only Fate could have dictated.

Such mixtures of savagery and grotesqueness mark other plays of this final period, from the other one-act pieces collected with *Ligazón* in *Retablo de la avaricia, la lujuria y la muerte* (Altar-piece of Avarice, Lust and Death) (1927), *La cabeza del Bautista* (*The Head of the Baptist*) (1924), *La rosa de papel* (*The Paper Rose*) (1924), and *Sacrilegio* (*Sacrilege*) (1927),[11] to the full-length works in *Martes de carnaval*[12] (Shrove Tuesday) (1930): *Los cuernos de don Friolera* (The Horns of Don Friolera) (1925), *Las galas del difunto* (The Corpse's Regalia) (1930), *La hija del capitán* (The Captain's Daughter) (1927). Each of these plays is an *esperpento*, whether designated as such or not, and each handles the social ills and hypocrisy addressed in the grotesque manner typical of the genre.

Such ideas as expressed in *Luces de bohemia* regarding the *esperpento* were augmented in *Esperpento de los cuernos de don Friolera*. In a dialogue during the play's prologue, Don Estrafalario states:

Tears and laughter are born out of the contemplation of things akin to ourselves ... We reserve our jeers for whatever relates to us ... My aesthetic transcends pain and sorrow, as must the conversations of the dead when they tell stories of the living. All our art is born out of the knowledge that we will pass away some day.[13]

The play, in which the military is burlesqued in the context of the anti-hero's cuckolding and his reluctance to confront the situation as mandated by the officers's code of honour, provides the dramatist with an opportunity to apply 'the mathematics of the concave mirror' to yet another sacrosanct institution and thus ridicule its members and its rules. Other variants on the theme are dealt with in *Las galas del difunto* and *La hija del capitán*.

The dramatist continued to amplify the aesthetic of the *esperpento* in such plays, as well as through the opportunities presented him by numerous interviews. In one of these interviews he made an important addition to the premises that informed his vision:

Life – its events, sorrows, loves – is always the same, fatally so. What changes are the characters, the protagonists of life. Those roles were previously played by gods and heroes.

---

[11] For a study of these plays, see my article 'Melodramas for Puppets and Playlets for Silhouettes: Four Stageworks by Valle-Inclán', *Modern Drama* (Kansas), XIII, no. 4, February 1971, pp. 374–381. The plays in English are collected in Ramón del Valle-Inclán, *Savage Acts. Four Plays*, translated by Robert Lima (University Park: Estreno Contemporary Spanish Plays Series, 1993).

[12] The title is a pun that could be translated as 'Shrove Tuesday' or, in keeping with the subject matter of the collection – anti-militarism – either 'Martial Carnival' or 'A Carnavalesque Mars'. In keeping with the spirit of Goya, I have chosen the more traditional translation.

[13] Ramón del Valle-Inclán, *Esperpento de los cuernos de don Friolera* (Madrid: Espasa-Calpe, 1969), prologue. The translation is mine.

... In the past, destiny fell on the shoulders – haughtiness and sorrow – of Oedipus or Medea. Today, destiny is the same, fate is the same, greatness is the same, pain is the same ... But the shoulders that bear them have changed. Actions, concerns, recognition are the same as yesterday and forever. The shoulders are different, too miniscule to support the weight. Out of that are born contrast, disproportion, and the ridiculous. In *Los cuernos de don Friolera*, the sorrow of the protagonist is the same as Othello's and yet it lacks its greatness. Blindness is beautiful and noble in Homer. But in *Luces de bohemia* the same blindness is sad and lamentable because it concerns a bohemian poet, Máximo Estrella.[14]

But society as a whole is really no different at the end of these plays. Those people who have died have left behind an unchanging scheme of life in which some will continue to suffer greatly, some will show no pity, being moved only by fear, some will continue as they were, perhaps to again manifest their fallen nature through outright evil or extreme selfishness.

Society is savaged by Valle-Inclán in *Luces de bohemia, Divinas palabras*, and *Ligazón*, as well as in the other *esperpentos*, because the dramatist views society as hypocritical, self-serving, and abusive of power. Because it perpetrates and condones savage acts that not only mock the Christian charity it purportedly espouses but also the protective parameters of ethical behavior, society is deservedly savaged by the acidic attack it receives in each *esperpento*, be it set in rural Galicia or urban Madrid, be it concerned with naive primitive traditions or sophisticated modern protocols. It is Valle-Inclán's sense that an absurd, depraved, corrosive society deserves to be depicted as such.

Much of Spanish post-Civil War drama has been influenced by his innovative ideas in writing and staging plays, as has been acknowledged by Antonio Buero Vallejo, Alfonso Sastre, José Martín Recuerda, Antonio Gala, Domingo Miras, Carlos Muñiz, and Francisco Nieva, among other prominent contemporary playwrights. Buero, for one, has said of Valle-Inclán's most immediate influence that:

he fecundates the greatest dramatist that follows: Lorca. And today he manifests himself as a unique author, a formidable revealer of his land and of the sullen or ludicrous face that speaks the truth about man: that truth, among others, that shows man as a marionette subject to his conditioned reflexes.[15]

And Sastre has placed him at the centre of the modern European theatre:

Valle-Inclán is one of the great masters of the European theatre of this century ... His theatre represents the autonomous Spanish discovery of theatrical expressionism; the anticipation of

---

[14] Francisco Madrid, *La vida altiva de Valle-Inclán*, p. 114. The translation is mine.
[15] 'Encuesta sobre el teatro de Valle-Inclán', *Insula* (Madrid), XVI, nos. 176–177, July–August 1961, p. 4. The translation is mine.

the antipsychologicalism of the subsequent 'social' theatre, and the deliberate use of the technique of 'distancing' (which Brecht would come to use and explicate theoretically).[16]

With the *esperpento* Valle-Inclán established the tenets and techniques that mark his plays as precursors of the later and much-touted Theatre of the Absurd. Although the Irishman Beckett, the Rumanian Ionesco, and the Spaniard Arrabal, among others, have received greater kudos, Valle-Inclán's creativity as a playwright has come to be acknowledged as his plays found their way into the repertory, having been translated into all the major Western languages.[17] Today, his plays are performed throughout the European continent, Spanish America, the United States, and elsewhere. In 1963 two of his most important works were presented in Paris: *Divines paroles* (*Divine Words*), directed by Roger Blin at the Odéon with Jean-Louis Barrault, and *Lumières de Bohême* (*Bohemian Lights*), directed by Roger Wilson, who also performed in the lead role. Notable among recent productions are those directed by Jorge Lavelli (*Comédies barbares*) (Savage Plays), Lluís Pasqual (*Luces de bohemia; Tirano Banderas* [The Tyrant Banderas], adapted from the novel), and Víctor García (*La rosa de papel; Divinas palabras*, with Núria Espert).

More so than ever before, Valle-Inclán's importance as an innovative dramatist in his own right and as the Spanish precursor of the absurdist mode in theatre has come to be recognized in the present period both by critics and directors worldwide.

Valle-Inclán's Plays in English Translation

Aguila de blasón
   Heraldic Eagle. Translated by Asa Katz. In *Barbaric Comedies*. New York: Marsilio, Forthcoming.

La cabeza del Bautista
   The Head of the Baptist. Translated by Robert Lima. In *Savage Acts. Four Plays*. University Park: Estreno Contemporary Spanish Plays, 1993, pp. 33–48.

La cabeza del dragón
   The Dragon's Head. A Fantastic Farse. Translated by May Heywood Broun. In *Poet Lore* (Boston), XXIX, no. 5, 1918, pp. 531–564. Also in *Poet Lore Plays*, Series 2. Boston: R.G. Badger, 1919.

---

[16] *Ibid.* The translation is mine. I have used 'distancing' to convey the Spanish 'distanciamiento'. Brecht's technique is better known as the alienatory effect or alienation.
[17] See my *The International Annotated Bibliography of Ramón del Valle-Inclán: Volume I: Editions* (London: Grant & Cutler, Ltd, 1997).

Cara de Plata

Silver Face. Translated by Maria M. Delgado. In *Valle-Inclán Plays: One.* London: Methuen, 1993, pp. 185–273.

Silver Face. Translated by Asa Katz. In *Barbaric Comedies.* New York: Marsilio, Forthcoming.

Comedia de ensueño

Dream Comedy. Translated by Murray Paskin and Robert O'Brien. In *La Voz* (New York), VI, no. 2, November 1961, pp. 7–9.

Dream Comedy. Translated by Rosemary Shevlin Weiss. In *Doubles, Demons, and Dreamers. An International Collection of Symbolist Drama.* Ed. Daniel Gerould. New York: Performing Arts Journal Publications, 1985, pp. 139–145.

Los cuernos de don Friolera

The Horns of Don Friolera. Translated by Bryant Creel. In *Modern International Drama* (Binghamtom, NY), XX, no. 2, Spring 1987, pp. 29–68.

The Grotesque Farce of Mr. Punch the Cuckold. Translated by Robin Warner and Dominic Keown. Warminster: Aris & Phillips Ltd, 1991.

Divinas palabras

Divine Words (First Scene). Translated by Samuel Putnam. In *The European Caravan.* New York: Brewer, Warren & Putnam, 1931, pp. 332–336.

Divine Words. Translated by Edwin Williams. In, *Modern Spanish Theatre.* Eds. George Wellwarth and Michael Benedikt. New York: Dutton, 1968, pp. 1–78.

Divinas palabras (*Divine Words*). Translated by Trader Faulkner. London: Heinemann–London Theatre, 1977.

Divine Words. A Village Tragicomedy. Translated by Maria M. Delgado. In *Valle-Inclán Plays: One.* London: Methuen, 1993, pp. 1–89.

Ligazón

Blood Pact. Translated by Robert Lima. In *Modern International Drama* (Binghamton, NY), XXIV, no. 2, Spring 1991, pp. 65–74.

Blood Pact. Translated by Robert Lima. In Ramón del Valle-Inclán, *Savage Acts. Four Plays.* University Park: Estreno Contemporary Spanish Plays, 1993, pp. 1–15.

Luces de bohemia

Lights of Bohemia. Esperpento. Translated by Gerald Gillespie and Anthony N. Zahareas. *Kenyon Review* (Gambier, OH), XXIX, no. 5, November 1967, pp. 614–660.

Luces de bohemia. Bohemian Lights. Translated by Anthony N. Zahareas and Gerald Gillespie. Austin: University of Texas Press, 1976 and Edinburgh Bilingual Library, 10.

Bohemian Lights. Translated by David Johnston. Unpublished version set in 1915 Dublin for the 1993 production at the Gate Theatre, London.

Bohemian Lights. Esperpento. Translated by Maria M. Delgado. In *Valle-Inclán Plays: One*. London: Methuen, 1993, pp. 91–184.

Lights of Bohemia. Translated by John Lyon. Warminster: Aris & Philips, Ltd, 1994.

Romance de lobos

Wolves! Wolves! A Play of Savagery in Three Acts. Translated by Cyril Bertram Lander. Birmingham: C. B. Lander, 1957.

A Romance of Wolves. Translated by Asa Katz. In, *Barbaric Comedies*. New York: Marsilio, Forthcoming.

La rosa de papel

The Paper Rose. Translated by Robert Lima. In, *Savage Acts. Four Plays*. University Park: Estreno Contemporary Spanish Plays, 1993, pp. 17–32.

Sacrilegio

Sacrilege. Translated by Robert Lima. In *Savage Acts. Four Plays*. University Park: Estreno Contemporary Spanish Plays, 1993, pp. 49–61.

Contemporary Theatre Review
1998, Vol. 7, Part 2, pp. 47–59
Reprints available directly from the publisher
Photocopying permitted by license only

Drama, Religion and Republicanism: Theatrical Propaganda in the Spanish Civil War

James McCarthy

This article seeks to explore aspects of the role played by theatrical propaganda in the Republican zone during the Spanish Civil War. An attempt is made to place such theatrical activities in the wider context of Republican cultural activity before a detailed exploration is made of certain surviving texts in the light of their dramatic use of some ritual patterns, traditions and symbols of the Christian Church. Finally, the suggestion is made that this hitherto unresearched and little-regarded theatre can be seen as a unique element of Europe's radical political theatres such as those of Weimar Germany or the early Soviet Union.

KEY WORDS: *Teatro de urgencia* (*theatre of urgency*), Spanish theatre, Propaganda drama, Spanish Civil War.

The considerable research which has taken place in recent years to rediscover the Republican cultural activities of the Civil War has facilitated an increasingly detailed picture of a wide range of educational, artistic and social activity.[1] Literacy programmes, library provision, visual art exhibitions, schools creation and pedagogic campaigns in such diverse areas as science, music, hygiene and philosophy, are now well documented and testify to the Republic's evangelical fervour for 'the communication of culture in all its various aspects'.[2] Nor was it only amongst the civilian population that such efforts were made. Military

---

[1] See, for example, Hipólito Escolar, *La cultura durante la guerra civil* (Madrid: Alhambra, 1987) and *Valéncia, capital cultural de la República (1936–37): Antologia de textos i documents*, by Manuel Aznar Soler and others (Valencia: Generalitat Valenciana, 1986).

[2] *Memoria del patronato de Misiones Pedagógicas* (Madrid, 1933), p. xiv. The translation into English is my own, as are all subsequent translations.

training too was characterized not only by weapons handling and battlefield strategy, but also by cultural and political education. Recent research has also clarified the contribution which the theatre made to these latter activities through the short propaganda plays which were performed in improvised circumstances both in rearguard and frontline locations. This *teatro de urgencia* (*theatre of urgency*), as it has been described, effectively vanished after the Republic's defeat in 1939, but the gradual emergence of those works which survived in printed or manuscript form suggests that we can now view more clearly a distinct theatrical genre, hitherto largely neglected, but which played a signifi-cant cultural and military role in the war. Criticism of such theatre has been scant and predominantly confined to a brief general description of some essential characteristics. By contrast, in this short article I hope to initiate some new and more detailed areas of enquiry into this disre-garded aspect of Spanish cultural history, demonstrating how *teatro de urgencia* was a theatre much influenced by some of the ritual patterns, traditions and symbols of the Christian Church.[3]

Given the leading role of the Communists and Socialists in nurturing theatrical propaganda and its consequent Marxist emphasis, a link between such drama and the Church might seem improbable. In both cases, however, we are dealing with doctrines which have been, and continue to be, expounded with evangelical passion. Marxism and Christianity offer adherents an afterlife, although in the case of the former this is a certainty existing in a temporal future rather than a spiritual utopia beyond the material world. Bertrand Russell saw the links between Communism and Religion when he asserted that both went beyond or contrary to evidence, entering a realm of faith engen-dered not by intellectual means but by emotionalism or authoritarian-ism.[4] Ironically, therefore, while church and state were mutually antagonistic during much of the Republic's existence, as doctrinal propa-gandists they shared much in common. An illuminating example of this idea is found in *Tres soldados en una batalla* (*Three Soldiers in a Battle*), a play performed before Republican troops in the Gandesa sector during the spring of 1938.[5] Terrified by the heat of battle an unnamed soldier

---

[3] Much of the information in this article derives from doctoral research currently in progress. For further information about *teatro de urgencia* see Francisco Mundi Pedret, *El teatro en la guerra civil* (Barcelona: PPU, 1987) or James McCarthy, 'The Republican Theatre during the Spanish Civil War: Rafael Alberti's *Numancia*', *Theatre Research International*, 4, 1980, 193–205.

[4] Bertrand Russell, *The Practice and Theory of Communism* (London: Macmillan, 1954), p. 13.

[5] *Tres soldados en una batalla*, in *Un teatro de guerra* (Madrid–Barcelona: Editorial Nuestro Pueblo, 1938), pp. 89–95. Page references, for this and all subsequent plays, are given after quotations in the text.

finds comfort in the exemplary courage of his comrade, declaring: 'you give faith to one' (p. 93). The sentiment, coupled with the stage picture of three actors dressed like their audience, the simplest décor, the platform stage and an anonymous playwright, recalls the great medieval Mystery Cycles and the Morality plays, and links two kinds of theatre, secular and liturgical, modern and historical, binding them together through the crusading role of faith.[6] It is in the propagation of faith that we find the impulse both of *teatro de urgencia* and the church drama of the Middle Ages. In the modern example the soldier, and through him the citizen-spectator, is exhorted to belief and exemplary action through adherence to the secular religion of Republicanism. The deity becomes, rather than the Christian God, an amalgam of various totemic concepts which *teatro de urgencia* presents in solemn, semi-mystical terms: People, Land, Spain, the Workers' Republic and, as might be expected in a country which practises mariolatry, Mother.

Teatro de urgencia, thus, presents devotion to the Republic as the responsibility of all citizens and, as in medieval drama, the sense of the entire community being represented is strong. Yet, although a wide range of ages, classes and occupations is found in the genre, there is, perhaps inevitably in a theatre of this kind, a persistent concentration on the figure of the Republican soldier, the *miliciano*. In his doubts and fears, strength and hope, a collective Everyman figure emerges from the corpus of the texts and, just as his medieval counterpart undertook a journey towards the heaven of unification with God, so too can the *miliciano* be seen in *teatro de urgencia* at various stages of a journey towards an afterlife which is victory. Like Everyman, the *miliciano*, too, faces temptation, despair and confusion on his journey and, like the medieval character, he serves as a representative example to the audience of the need to embrace Good Deeds, in this case through unflinching commitment to the war effort.

The sense of the soul or pilgrim initiating a journey towards God is keenly felt in Aub's *Pedro López García* which was presented on a church altar during September 1936 in what seems to have been its only wartime performance.[7] The play traces the story of a young shepherd, Pedro, who is forcibly enlisted in the Nationalist army but, through the appearance before him in the trenches of two apparitions, those of his mother and La Tierra (Native Land), he finds the courage to cross to 'your brothers' trench' (p. 391). It is not only his commonplace name

---

[6] For information about medieval drama see Christine Richardson and Jackie Johnstone, *Medieval Drama* (London: Macmillan, 1991).

[7] Max Aub, *Pedro López García, Hora de España*, 19, 1938, pp. 81–100; repr. in *Hora de España*, 5 vols (Liechtenstein: Detlev Auvermann, 1977), 4, pp. 373–392.

which suggests that Pedro López García is intended as an Everyman figure, since, as his medieval counterpart never imagined that Death would visit him so soon, Pedro has not imagined that the war will visit his mountain hut. Pedro is, in effect, a non-believer at the start of the play, rejecting the idea that the war or the Republic impinge on his life. The distant explosions of artillery provoke prayer from his mother but a shrug of the shoulders from Pedro. For him: 'to each his own' (p. 377). Yet, as Death visits Everyman, so too it visits Pedro in the form of a brutal Nationalist sergeant who murders Pedro's mother, kills his animals and steals him away from the land which he had imagined as paradise:

All that matters to me is that my animals are contented. When I walk them on the mountain I end up thinking that I too am the land and that's why they come with me so happily and eat from my hand (p. 377).

In the second scene of the play, which takes place on a dark night in the Nationalist trenches, a Republican loudspeaker addresses the rebel soldiers, urging them to rediscover 'faith in the high destinies of the nation' (p. 387) by crossing to loyal Spain. Such disembodied voices exhorting soldiers to correct action are frequent in *teatro de urgencia*. Characterized as, for example, The Voice of the People (La voz del pueblo), The Voice of Spain (La voz de España) or The Voice of the Poet (La voz del poeta), their role is that of the abstract deity who speaks to the tangible world, expounding and urging the doctrine of Republicanism. In Aub's play the church setting is particularly significant for this voice since the staging can enhance, through spatial levels, the notion of the trench as hell, Pedro as lost soul and the voice as emanating from the divine wisdom of heaven.

The voice's call to action is followed by a moment of epiphany for Pedro, a vision which deepens the play's religious overtones. It is a moment which sees the gradual loss of rational faculties and an emotional, almost mystical affirmation in the manner of a spiritual revelation. Initially, the apparition of his mother debates with him, urging the need to commit himself, to recognize the power and right of those in the opposing trench, to overcome his fear 'that they might kill me, that I might be killed by the one who stands guard there so that I cannot pass, the same as I watch him so that he might not do it' (p. 389). The soldier weighs his options and finds the risks too great. His conversation with the ghost of his mother ends in impasse, in the brusque communication which characterized their relationship before her death:

MOTHER: You are the prisoner of yourself. You are a coward.
PEDRO: Why do you say things you don't mean? I am your son (p. 389).

The appearance, however, of La Tierra, declaring 'I am the Beginning and the End' (p. 389), deepens the crisis of commitment for Pedro, moving him beyond rational considerations of strategic survival. As his mother's spirit enfolds itself in the figure's skirts, he seems incapable of recognizing a figure which, both in terms of its language and its Madonna-like appearance on the altar, seems to speak with divine authority: 'outside of me nothing exists and your heart and your mouth and your teeth and your tongue have been born of me' (p. 390). Unable to comprehend the figure's call to see himself as part of 'what matters, what is, what exists' (p. 389), Pedro moves beyond rational questioning and embraces faith through emotional surrender: 'I haven't understood what you're telling me. But I believe I must desert' (p. 391). As the apparitions vanish Pedro climbs the parapet and the play closes with, as it were, the god speaking through him as he now uses the loudspeaker to call the names of those who remain in the rebel trenches, urging them to similar resolution.

Pedro López García becomes a believer in one particularly significant manner, that he does not require evidence upon which to base his belief. The juxtaposition of the verbs *believe* (*creer*) and *ought* (*deber*) at the decisive moment calls attention to a characteristic quality both of the *miliciano* and the Christian devotee: duty impelled by faith. The Mother has recognized this spiritual quality in the first scene when she tells the Sergeant that her son can never fight against the *pueblo* because 'something will rise up within him and prevent it' (p. 379). This deep bond with the *pueblo* is, in Christian terms, akin to the believer's relationship with God, and just as the Church, through prayer, confession and teaching, seeks to confirm this bond at moments of crisis or failure, so too does *teatro de urgencia* work to strengthen the believer when faith lapses, temptation intervenes or commitment wanes. Again, one is reminded of Everyman, or indeed Bunyan's Pilgrim, in that the most difficult aspect of faith is its practice in daily life. For the Republican propagandists, therefore, it is as if, having won Pedro López García to the loyalist trenches, their subsequent mission is to translate his faith into deeds when, reappearing as the collective character of the *miliciano* in subsequent *teatro de urgencia*, he continues on a journey in which spiritual conviction is emphasized more than material comfort.

Such a task is less apparent in Aub's play since, written in the initial weeks of the war, its predominant tone is the optimistic certainty of victory which seems to have characterized the mood of Republican Spain at this time. Gradually, however, the conflict's true nature presented itself to the Republic as an exhausting struggle against increasingly difficult odds. Theatrical propaganda undertook new approaches to aid this struggle and, within a kind of doctrinal framework, sought to provide appropriate and effective explanations for the *miliciano* not just of the need, like Pedro López García, to find faith but, perhaps more importantly, the need, despite every setback, to maintain such faith.

It is striking how, in attempting this political task, and across a range of named or anonymous writers who were largely unknown to each other, Christian practices and symbolism, particularly theatrical aspects, continue to play a significant role. In 1937, for example, the Comisariado General de Guerra (General Commissariat of War) published the *Meditación del miliciano* (*Meditation of the Soldier*), an alphabetically-arranged volume of philosophical, spiritual and religious quotations intended for individual or collective reflection.[8] The *miliciano* is directed to ponder, for example, Good and Evil (Bien y Mal), Morality (Moralidad) and Religion (Religión) alongside War (Guerra), Communism (Comunismo), Anarchism (Anarquismo) and Politics (Política), in a format which recalls scriptural study or the Roman Catholic concept of periodic retreat for spiritual nourishment. In the drama which emanated from the General Commissariat of War further Christian parallels are found. For example, in *La voz de España* (*The Voice of Spain*) and *La muerte y la vida* (*Death and Life*) the medieval theatre figure of the Devil or Vice is strongly suggested.[9] In the first play this character is presented as El Fascista (The Fascist), grotesquely masked and furtively tempting the *miliciano*. His victim has succumbed to drunkenness, is irresolute in his commitment to the struggle and, thus, susceptible to the devil's whispered suggestions:

> Go to the front? What madness!
> Make superhuman excuses,
> Don't fight or expose yourself to danger;
> Be sly, sly and sensible.
> The war is already lost,
> Very soon Franco's going to arrive (p. 27).

At this point, in the traditional manner of evil figures in the Mystery Cycles, he confides his real intentions to the spectators: 'then I'll seize you and strangle you with my own hands' (p. 27). Such a character reappears in the second play, this time as Death but disguised, like El Fascista, 'as grotesquely as possible' (p. 5). Again, the victim is the *miliciano* whom Death approaches: 'about to grasp him in his claws' (p. 7). However, as the play's title suggests, the *miliciano's* faith is now resolute and, triumphant, he challenges Death and, perhaps in a conscious inversion of the story of Jesus' temptation in the desert, the devil figure is made to survey loyalist Spain:

---

[8] *Meditación del miliciano* (Barcelona: Editorial Labor, 1937).

[9] José Herrera Petere, *La voz de España*, in *Teatro para combatientes* (Valencia(?): Subcomisariado de Agitación, Prensa y Propaganda, 1937); repr. (Madrid: Editorial Hispamerca, 1977), pp. 25–31 and *La muerte y la vida*, in *En las trincheras* (Valencia(?): Subcomisariado de Agitación, Prensa y Propaganda, (1937?)), pp. 5–8.

And he sees children in the cities
with joy on their faces
thinking about the future
of a liberated Spain.
And sees the work in the villages,
and in the fields and mountains,
and a whole people who long
to see their chains broken (p. 7).

As Antichrist and the fallen angels were banished from the medieval plays with screams and howls, helpless before the power of faith, so here Death shrinks from the stage in shame, 'with cries of horror' (p. 7).

Although these two plays work, like much medieval theatre, on the level of abstraction, similar resonances of liturgical drama can be found in *teatro de urgencia* which portrays army life in a manner more grounded in realism. Particularly noticeable is the frequency with which a dispirited or inactive *miliciano* listens to an extensive monologue from his more dedicated comrade. Effectively a sermon, this clarifies Republican doctrine by reiterating duty in word and deed. As the virtuous life was illustrated in medieval theatre by similar dramatic methods and was often expounded by sanctified figures, the resolute *miliciano* can be seen in such speeches in the role of priest and his monologue as a sermon intended not only for the other characters on the stage, but also for the spectators who now find themselves in the role of congregation. In *Mi puesto está en las trincheras* (*My Place is in the Trenches*), for example, a *miliciano* is upbraided for his lack of Republican fervour:[10]

I would like your attitude to be different. You seem to me passive, reluctant, lacking in spirit always ... You don't fight joyfully ... You are embittered, withdrawn, timid ... You never laugh, you never sing ... I don't believe you're a bad young chap, but I do believe that you haven't yet learnt what an honour it is for us to be a soldier in the Freedom Army (p. 8).

Like a sermon the speech urges a way of living which celebrates doctrine, in this case what the *miliciano* suggests is the liberating task of forging 'a new world, laws which will favour the workers' (p. 6). A similar example is found in Hernández's *Los sentados* (*The Seated Ones*)[11] where frivolity and lack of interest in the war are berated by the *miliciano* who accuses his comrades of being 'completely oblivious of the blood which our comrades are spilling' (p. 829) and exhorts them to 'walk with a rifle to defend yourself from tyranny and hunger' (p. 829). This

---

[10] Luis Mussot, 'Mi puesto está en las trincheras', unpublished ms. in my possession.
[11] Miguel Hernández, *Los sentados*, in *Obras completas* (Buenos Aires: Losada, 1973), pp. 827–832.

essentially static dramatic technique, the monologue, abounds in *teatro de urgencia*, uniting both pulpit and soap box in a structured harangue which seeks to encourage the reaffirmation of faith, the eager acceptance of duty and a political vision of the war's justness.

It is significant that, while Aub's play was written for the student theatre company, El Búho, the other plays I have discussed were written in military circumstances and intended, as part of the Republican effort to build an efficient army from the popular militias, to teach combatants highly specific lessons about appropriate behaviour. The plays which were written or requested by political commissars in army units form, therefore, a kind of Republican catechism, illustrating military and political correctness through unambiguous example. In *Mi puesto está en las trincheras*, for example, the *miliciano*, again assuming the role of priest, tests the congregation's orthodoxy when the audience is asked to respond to a series of questions, such as: 'don't you agree that a people such as ours can never be enslaved?' (p. 9) and 'don't you agree that the crushing of the enemy will signify the independence of the fatherland?' (p. 9). A similar idea is found in Narezo's *¡Hacia la victoria!* (*Towards Victory!*)[12] when the character of the Comisario opens the play, 'addressing the audience rather than the actors' (p. 3), by posing the question which the drama then answers through doctrinal example: 'a question which you will often have asked yourselves: why do our soldiers abandon their posts and run?' (p. 3).

If Aub's play demonstrates the awakening of faith, these subsequent plays seek to indicate the path of righteousness and show the *miliciano* in his struggles to enact the Republican creed in his daily life. In Bleiberg's *Amanecer* (*Dawn*),[13] for example, physical hardship, cold and self-sacrifice are embraced with optimism as the route to 'the new Spain which our rifles are forging' (p. 130), and in Herrera Petere's *Torredonjil*, the *miliciano* overcomes his pride and greed, learning to respect and aid his rural comrades:[14]

> Torredonjil, your crops,
> your bundles of rye
> I'll gather with my hands
> black with powder and fire (p. 23).

Faith, thus, combines with hope and charity to become both Christian and Republican virtues, active qualities which *teatro de urgencia* reiterates

---

[12] Gabriel Narezo, *¡Hacia la victoria!* (Valencia(?): Subcomisariado de Propaganda, (1937?)).
[13] Germán Bleiberg, *Amanecer*, in *Teatro de agitación política* (Madrid: Editorial Cuadernos para el Diálogo, 1977), pp. 105–132.
[14] José Herrera Petere, *Torredonjil*, in *Teatro para combatientes* (Valencia(?): Subcomisariado de Agitación, Prensa y Propaganda, 1937; repr. Madrid: Editorial Hispamerca, 1977), pp. 17–24.

as essential to victory and what is presented as the subsequent paradise of the new society.

The composition of Aub's play early in the war assumes further significance when we consider the attitude towards death which it presents. When La Tierra dismisses Pedro's fear, declaring death 'a simple thing of little import' (p. 390), it lacks the heroic grandeur with which later *teatro de urgencia* presented death when, at the end of his journey, the *miliciano* must learn that in the manner of his dying lies the means by which he can approach and be welcomed by his God. Notions of death as martyrdom, example and sacrifice intensify the Christian qualities of the drama and, in the imagery which surrounds the character of the *miliciano*, that of shepherd, priest and common man, lies the suggestion of the soldier as Son of God and that in his passion and martyrdom he is reunited with a deity who has asked the utmost of him.

Such an idea is strongly emphasized in Bleiberg's *Sombras de héroes* (*Shadows of Heroes*)[15] which opens with the funeral of a *miliciano* who was 'the last to abandon the position' (p. 138) and closes with the death of another *miliciano* who, similarly, has defended Euzkadi 'until death' (p. 163). In the opening scene the *milicianos* who shovel earth into the grave find example rather than mourning in their comrade's death and there is the sense that in his ending he returns to, and is embraced by, the Republican trinity of People, Land and Spain. Thus, he has died with the name of Spain on his lips, his body rests in Basque soil and 'the soil from which you sprang covers you today in glory' (p. 138).

Such a heroic view of death is reiterated in the final scene, but also shown is the *miliciano*'s confusion and wavering resolution. Alone and at night, with all his comrades dead, his frail humanity is contrasted with the demands about to be made upon him: 'Alone here. One rifle. Two arms. Two ears. Two eyes. One heart. And blood' (p. 160). Isolated and close to despair he calls upon his parents for comfort, sensing 'how close I feel you today, on this dark, cold night!' (p. 160). One is reminded of the agony of Gethsemane, not only in the fear of impending death, but also in the search for the strength to endure this ultimate testing of faith and duty. In terror he considers the denial of his faith through desertion: 'I know every road in Euzkadi ... I can leave the rifle and run towards Bilbao' (p. 160). As in *Pedro López García*, however, this precipitates a vision and he is confronted by the spirits of the Basque dead, victims of the bombing of Eibar, Durango and Guernica. The *pueblo*, as it were, appears before him, reminding him that it has sacrificed all. The spirit of La Mujer Vieja (The Old Woman) scorns his thoughts of running

---

[15] Germán Bleiberg, *Sombras de héroes*, in *Teatro de agitación política* (Madrid: Editorial Cuadernos para el Diálogo, 1977), pp. 133–164.

away when her blood itself has run through the streets of Eibar, 'and there I am still, forgotten amongst the ruins' (p. 160). As three more spirits of the *pueblo* recount their own sacrifice the *miliciano*, in his confusion and fear, attempts a denial of his faith: 'No! I don't know! I know nothing. Go back, spirits! Leave me!' (p. 161). Yet the spirits cannot be ignored since sacrifice is the crux of such faith and must here culminate in the words of the final vision, the Anciano (The Old Man), who, perhaps recalling both the *miliciano*'s father and God the Father, urges him to 'fight, Basque soldier, fight until you conquer or die' (p. 162). His subsequent death in the closing moments of the play is seen, like Christ's passion following Gethsemene, as a sacrifice to redeem the land, suggesting that those who follow will find example in his martyrdom: 'and if Bilbao fell to German power, the world will understand it was not through Basque cowardice. And I know that the men of Spain will know how to avenge this crime' (p. 163). His heroism is rewarded with an oration from the god as La voz del pueblo enters and, emphasizing the *miliciano*'s role as exemplary symbol of the collective's faith, extends the action's meaning out into the audience:

Spain has an army!
The dead heroes shout:
victory is ours alone! (p. 164).

In the manner of his death the *miliciano* shows himself able, like Everyman, to take Good Deeds down to the grave with him. In turn this elevates the soldier to a place at the side of his God. Such an idea is richly explored in Alberti's *La cantata de los héroes y la fraternidad de los pueblos* (*The Cantata of the Heroes and the Fraternity of Peoples*) where the various icons which constitute the Republican deity: mother, Spain, the people, fraternal love and heroic sacrifice, fuse together to honour and embrace the *miliciano*.[16] In the *Cantata de los héroes* this occurs in a form so heavily dominated by Christian ritual that it blurs the distinction between theatrical event and sacred ceremony, seeking to encapsulate in verse the Republic's doctrine of the war. Initially, two Recitantes (Narrators) conduct the audience through an account of Spain's landscape which is presented as Eden disrupted by 'treason and disgrace' (p. 185). Summoning España, she stands between two soldiers from the opposing camps and mourns her rebel son since 'in my throat you place a lament of chains' (p. 187) by abandoning her to the 'hybrid beasts' (p. 189) of Germany and Italy. In contrast, she now welcomes other foreigners, this

---

[16] Rafael Alberti, *La cantata de los héroes y la fraternidad de los pueblos*, in *Teatro* (Buenos Aires: Bajel, 1942), pp. 180–201.

time 'the flower of the world' (p. 190), the soldiers of the International Brigades who enter bearing flags and offer themselves to the service of Spain. As the soldiers are embraced, the narrators offer 'glory and honour to the dead' (p. 192), incanting the names of the dead brigaders. Such praise is intensified as the Mujeres españolas (Spanish Women) enter, led by the Madre, who declares: 'you will live within us, vigilant night and day, as if you were buried in our breast' (p. 195). As the brigaders leave they place their flags at the feet of España, but she is not abandoned since *milicianos* now enter, solemnly receiving the flags from the hands of the women. Stricken with remorse and sudden insight the rebel soldier now recognizes his error, kneeling for confession and forgiveness. Reunited, this prodigal son is incorporated into the lines of soldiers as España's mourning vestments are removed and La Fraternidad de los pueblos appears to join 'the oppressed hands of all nations' (p. 200). With the descent of flowers and the flight of doves the ritual ends in a processional exit, the narrators closing their books and turning from their lecterns as the curtain falls.

Arising from a tradition both of secular and sacred music, the *Cantata de los héroes* employs orchestral and vocal selections to punctuate the action and amplify its emotional significance. Yet, the role of music gives way to the much more powerful sense of theatre exploiting Christian symbolism. The setting emphasizes this by using small steps and columns to denote not so much a playing space as an altar, an impression which is enhanced by the presence of lecterns. The processional entrance of the First and Second Recitantes, each solemnly carrying a volume, intensifies the feeling of church service. The sense is that the volumes contain not so much the script of the cantata but sacred text. Christian iconography and ritual are also felt in the use of vestments, as when España's funeral robes are ceremoniously removed, in the audience standing to receive the International Brigades and in the rebel soldier's kneeling for absolution.

The powerful female presence, furthermore, moves us beyond merely Christian ritual, evoking images of the Catholic cult of the Madonna and the Mass. The Madre, España, the first Recitante and the group of women play roles which mingle those of priest and revealed deity. Thus, we find the female Recitante guiding the audience through what becomes a litany, reading from the lectern, but handing this priest role over to the Madre and the women who, in an action reminiscent of Catholic communion, deliver to the soldiers the International Brigade flags:

Mothers' hands, women's hands
pass them to you. May their
exemplary memory always wave
in the winds of patriotic stars and suns (p. 197).

It is a moment of great significance, blending ideas of benediction by some holy icon and the transmission of the sacrament and it provokes in the rebel soldier that recognition, frequently found in *teatro de urgencia*, which holds the political and the religious in fine balance:

> What a crime! What pain! Oh, what deceiving
> darkness they put in my eyes!
> You alone are the true Spain,
> the land of true Spaniards (p. 197).

It is as though divine revelation has occurred and it is important in this respect that the language and imagery which surround the character of España evoke the cult of Our Lady. Thus, España is spoken of in terms of dawn and the heart, of being 'the most fortunate sea' (p. 198), as 'the morning star' (p. 198) and, whereas at the opening of the cantata her heart was felt to be pierced by nails, at the end the traditional bleeding heart of the Madonna has been so transformed that 'from my breasts spring two rivers of hope!' (p. 201).

The ending of the *Cantata de los héroes* seems to encapsulate the whole meaning of the journey which the *miliciano* has taken since the awakening of Republican faith in Pedro López García, through the difficult lessons of war to the sacrifice of death and, as Everyman is taken up into heaven, a similar destiny awaits the *miliciano* as he is embraced at the end of the cantata by a deity who fuses the roles of people, mother, land and republic. In the final moments España, both as priest and object of worship, calls for the women and then the soldiers to speak 'the most tender and profound of all words' (p. 201). As though in prayer, each group in turn utters the word 'comrade' (p. 201), a concluding moment which illustrates *teatro de urgencia*'s clearest fusion of drama, religion and republicanism.

The defeat of the Republic in early 1939 and the subsequent dictatorship effectively removed all traces of theatrical innovation during the wartime years. The perception has arisen, therefore, that the period 1936–1939 was a hiatus in the Spanish theatre before 'normal' activities resumed with the end of hostilities.[17] Yet, while newspaper columns and contemporary testimony indicate the thriving persistence of the commercial theatre during these years,[18] the evidence of *teatro de urgencia* demonstrates that an alternative theatre sought to establish itself, one which was utilitarian, politically committed and which self-consciously

---

[17] See, for example, F. García Pavón, *El teatro social en España* (Madrid: Taurus, 1962), pp. 117–119.
[18] See, for example, R. Marrast, *El teatre durant la guerra civil espanyola* (Barcelona: Institut del Teatre, 1978).

rejected bourgeois notions of art. For many writers, Alberti and Aub prominent amongst them, such a theatre was an essential component, not just of tentatively evolving radical ideas about culture, but of the military victory without which such ideas could not flourish. *Teatro de urgencia* represents, therefore, Spain's contribution to that European political theatre of the earlier twentieth century which has been so well-documented in Britain, Germany and Russia, but which has been hitherto lost to Spain itself.[19] Further research needs to be done to reconstitute theatrical and dramatic aspects of *teatro de urgencia* but I hope to have illuminated significant aspects of the religious language and themes which permeate much of this drama and which suggest a variety not traditionally expected from agitprop theatre.[20]

---

[19] For information about similar dramatic experiments elsewhere in Europe see, for example, D. Bradby and J. McCormick, *People's Theatre* (London: Croom Helm, 1978) and M. Patterson, *The Revolution in German Theatre: 1900–1933* (London: Routledge, 1981). For information about political theatre in the USA see, for example, I. A. Levine, *Left-Wing Dramatic Theory in the American Theatre* (Ann Arbor: UMI, 1984).

[20] This article was first read at a research seminar in the Department of Hispanic Studies, University of Wales, Swansea. I am extremely grateful to members of the department for their numerous suggestions and advice.

Contemporary Theatre Review
1998, Vol. 7, Part 2, pp. 61–80
Reprints available directly from the publisher
Photocopying permitted by license only

Beyond Lorca

Martha T. Halsey and Phyllis Zatlin

This critical overview begins with a discussion of recent stagings of Lorca and Valle-Inclán and then focuses on the theatre of the post-Civil War period: comedies frequently revived in the 1980s and 1990s; the tragedies of Sastre and Buero Vallejo, Spain's foremost living playwright; the social plays of the 'Realistic Generation' which began to be performed in the 1960s; and the avant-garde pieces of 'underground' writers of the same period as well as of Paris-based Arrabal and of Nieva, the most successful proponent of non-representational theatre within Spain. The overview continues with the plays of Salom, Gala, and others such as Diosdado, Spain's woman author with the longest successful theatrical career, and concludes with the works of new playwrights who gained national recognition in democratic Spain: Alonso de Santos and Fermín Cabal, as well as several women playwrights who include Pedrero and Reina.

KEY WORDS: Twentieth-century Spanish drama, Theatre in post-Civil War Spain, Theatre in Franco and post-Franco Spain, The Madrid stage in the twentieth century.

Lorca lives. Although the world famous author, Federico García Lorca (1898–1936), was assassinated at the beginning of the Spanish Civil War, his theatre did not die with him. His plays continue to be staged internationally, and in new translations have achieved triumphs exceeding those during the Andalusian poet and playwright's lifetime. Among highly visible productions of the 1980s were Núria Espert's *La casa de Bernarda Alba* (*The House of Bernarda Alba*) in London and Jorge Lavelli's *El público* (*The Audience*) in Paris. Espert, working with a stellar cast headed by Glenda Jackson and Joan Plowright, was named best director of 1986 for her staging of Lorca's tragedy. In 1988 Lavelli inaugurated his tenure as artistic director of the Théâtre National de la Colline with *Le Public*, Lorca's daring, surrealistic defence of anti-bourgeois theatre and homosexual love which had remained unpublished and unstaged for decades after the author's death.

Valle-Inclán, too, lives, and his posthumous success story in some ways eclipses that of Lorca. While Lorca's existing fame as a playwright was enhanced by his tragic death, Ramón del Valle-Inclán (1866–1936) was seldom staged in Spain during his lifetime and little known outside the Spanish-speaking world. Indeed, his most innovative works for the theatre – including his expressionistic, cinematographic *esperpentos* (grotesque tragicomedies) – like Lorca's *El público*, were once considered unperformable. Only gradually has the older playwright become recognized as a major European dramatist who anticipated Brecht, Artaud, and the Theatre of the Absurd.

Valle-Inclán's *Luces de bohemia* (*Bohemian Lights*), first published in 1920, did not receive its world premiere until 1963. That Paris production, directed by Jean Vilar at the Théâtre National Populaire, coincided with Roger Blin's staging of *Divinas palabras* (*Divine Words*) at the Odéon; nevertheless, his international stature was firmly established only years later by touring Spanish-language companies. In the 1990s major stagings in Paris and London have met with critical and audience acclaim: Lavelli's 1991–1992 French version of Valle's epic trilogy, *Comedias bárbaras* (*Barbaric Comedies*); a 1993 adaptation at the Gate Theatre which transplanted the action of *Luces de bohemia* from Madrid to Dublin in 1915.

Such recent triumphs of Lorca and Valle-Inclán bring renewed attention to twentieth-century Spanish theatre and hence remove in part the curtain of silence that separated post-war Spain from other national stages during the long Franco regime (1939–1975). On the other hand, the growing reputation of these authors from the pre-war period does little to dispel the myth that Spanish theatre died with Lorca, that the land south of the Pyrenees has produced no new playwrights of interest in the past half century. Certainly it is true that the death or exile of many of Spain's greatest talents in the years surrounding the Spanish Civil War, as well as the censorship and political repression associated with a dictatorship, stifled creativity and freedom of expression, but theatre in Franco's Spain was neither moribund nor monolithic. It encompassed a full range of theatrical offerings from farce to tragedy, from traditional to inventive, from masterful to forgettable, from defence of the status quo to political protest.

Ironically, in the latest phase of the Spanish stage under democracy – one that is hopefully now drawing to a close in the 1994–1995 season – living Spanish authors have found themselves excluded from the most prestigious playhouses of their own country. The major government-subsidized theatres of Madrid have been in the process of rediscovering Lorca and Valle-Inclán while ignoring the writers in their midst. Yes, there is life after Lorca – but it hasn't always been an easy one. Speaking on behalf of a newly-organized playwrights' association, Alberto Miralles noted that during the 1990–1991 season the National Drama Centre (CDN) did not stage a single living Spanish writer.[1] Nor did the

---

[1] Alberto Miralles, 'Asociación de Autores de Teatro, en defensa propia', *Primer Acto*, no. 239, 1991, p. 134.

situation improve substantially in subsequent years. By the summer of 1994, CDN director José Carlos Plaza had been forced to resign. Perhaps Spanish playwrights are on the brink of a new era, but let us return to the history of the post-war stage.

In the years immediately following Franco's victory, Spanish theatre was dominated by conservative plays exalting Spain's history and myths, formulaic bourgeois dramas from the pen of ageing Nobel Prize-winner Jacinto Benavente (1866–1954), and comedies that liberal critics generally labeled 'escapist' – and hence presumably of no redeeming social or literary value. Nevertheless, many of the comedies from the 1940s and 1950s live on.

Among writers of comedy whose works are frequently revived in contemporary Spain are Enrique Jardiel Poncela (1901–1952) and Miguel Mihura (1905–1977). The former, whose unconventional humour gave rise to quasi-absurdist dialogue and wild parody, was doubtless Spain's most original playwright of the early post-war years. A revival at the CDN of *Eloísa está debajo de un almendro* (*Eloise Is Under an Almond Tree*), in a creative staging by Plaza that emphasized its ties to Hollywood films, was a major hit in 1984. Starting in 1980, with the mystery farce *Los habitantes de la casa deshabitada* (*The Inhabitants of the Uninhabited House*), Mara Recatero achieved considerable success in commercial playhouses with a series of Jardiel productions. Notable among these was *Un marido de idea y vuelta* (*A Round-trip Husband*) (1939) which ran for more than 500 performances in 1985. Central to the action is the return, in ghostly form, of a husband who is irate at his wife's remarriage; the story bears strong parallels to Noel Coward's later *Blithe Spirit*, (1941).

Mihura's most admired work, *Tres sombreros de copa* (*Three Top Hats*), was written in 1932 but not staged until 1952. On the eve of his marriage to a conventionally dull and demanding bourgeois wife, a young man flirts with the idea of running off with an attractive member of a travelling vaudeville company which has inexplicably invaded his hotel room. Clearly related to the European avant-garde, this tragicomic farce has been widely recognized as a precursor to the post-war Theatre of the Absurd. It gained for its author instant fame, and Mihura's comedies continue to be a part of national repertoire.

Another writer of comedies whose works remain of interest is José López Rubio (1903–1996). Like Víctor Ruiz Iriarte (1912–1982), whose *El landó de seis caballos* (*The Six-Horse Landau*) (1950) is considered the prototype of the post-war Spanish comedies of theatricalized life, López Rubio participates in an international current of metatheatrical comedy. The revival of López Rubio's *Celos del aire* (Trans. Marion P. Holt *In August We Play the Pyrenees*) (1950) met with such enthusiasm in 1990–1991 that when the production had to close at the municipal Centro Cultural de la Villa (Madrid's culture centre), it moved on for the rest of the season to a commercial playhouse; along with *La venda en los ojos* (*The Blindfold*) and *La otra orilla* (*The Other Shore*) (1954) it has been translated into English and staged in the United States. *Celos del aire*, dealing with a young wife's imaginary jealousy that turns out to be true, makes spectators within the play of an elderly couple who have rented part of their home but whimsically prefer to pretend that they and the tenants are mutually invisible. The result is an exceedingly clever metaplay that parodies its own well-made structure.

Historia de una escalera (*Story of a Stairway*) (1949) by Antonio Buero Vallejo (b. 1916) signalled a turning point on the post-war stage, marking the new direction to be taken by a growing number of younger playwrights who felt an obligation to focus on the problems of their society. Buero's drama portrayed the working-class people of a dilapidated Madrid tenement; the single setting of the unchanging stairway symbolized the fate of three successive generations who remained trapped in the same wretched situation. Incorporating a tragic portrayal of human existence generally absent from twentieth-century Spanish theatre, *Historia de una escalera* represented a passionate but lucid judgement on Spanish society of the period.

When *Historia de una escalera* opened, its author was virtually unknown. After fighting on the Republican side in the Civil War, he had spent seven years in prison. His play, submitted anonymously, had won Spain's coveted and most prestigious theatre award, the Lope de Vega Prize. Buero was eventually to become Spain's foremost contemporary playwright. For more than a decade his plays have been performed regularly in Russia, Germany, Poland, Hungary, Rumania, Czechoslovakia, Sweden, Finland, Norway, and other countries. With productions of his *El sueño de la razón* (*The Sleep of Reason*) in Baltimore, 1984, in Philadelphia, 1986, and in Chicago, 1994, Buero has also begun to reach the commercial American stage. In 1987 he became the first playwright to be awarded the Cervantes Prize, an honour frequently referred to as the Nobel Prize of the Hispanic world.

The opening of *Un soñador para un pueblo* (*A Dreamer for a People*) (1958) introduced to the Spanish stage a kind of historical theatre that examines the past critically. Buero's originality lay in the fact that he made historical distancing and emotive identification complementary functions of dramatic structure and established a dialectical synthesis between past and present. With the staging of *El tragaluz* (*The Basement Window*) (1967) and the English version of *La doble historia del doctor Valmy* (*The Double Case History of Doctor Valmy*) (1968) in Chester, England, Buero Vallejo introduced another new current, that of expressionistic, subjective drama. In *El sueño de la razón* he intensified this subjective point of view on stage while returning to his exploration of Spain's past.

The 1970 work, which portrays the ageing and deaf Goya in conflict with the tyrannical king Ferdinand VII, makes extensive use of what Ricardo Doménech has termed an 'immersion effect', a technique that has come to be associated with Buero's name.[2] The phrase refers to effects of psychic participation which allow the spectators to perceive reality through the perspective of a character or group of characters who suffer some type of physical defect or psychological abnormality. In *El sueño de la razón* Buero includes both possibilities: the audience shares Goya's deafness and his terrifying hallucinations. As with the earlier current of historical drama, Buero Vallejo's use of psychological expressionism has had an important influence on other Spanish playwrights.

La Fundación (*The Foundation*) (1974) and *El sueño de la razón*, together with the earlier *El Concierto de San Ovidio* (*The Concert at Saint Ovide*) (1962) are the plays which to date have brought Buero the most international acclaim. At the beginning of *La Fundación*, the action appears to take place in a room of an elegant centre for research with a picture window opening on a magnificent landscape. At the end, the spectators find themselves in a prison cell and discover that the characters are not eminent writers and scientists with grants from a 'Foundation' but political prisoners. The audience, although not realizing it until near the end of the drama, sees reality through the eyes of Tomás, a young prisoner who, unable to face reality, creates an illusory world. His gradual acceptance of the truth is represented visually by changes in stage decor as the pleasant furnishings of the 'Foundation' vanish to be replaced with the sordid trappings of a cell. Buero's play constituted an attack upon political systems that deceive and enslave, but the drama is also an expression of hope for a day in which a dark reality may be transformed into a luminous landscape seen by Tomás.

Painters and painting have played major roles in Buero Vallejo's theatre. In *Las Meninas* (1960) he used Velázquez's masterpiece to make a powerful statement about an epoch of oppression, of pretence and hypocrisy closely paralleling the Franco dictatorship. In *Diálogo secreto* (*Secret Dialogue*) (1984) he utilizes another Velázquez painting, 'The Spinners', to express the tragedy of his protagonist, a famed art critic who desperately conceals a terrible secret: he has always been colour-blind. As the latter gazes at the huge reproduction of 'The Spinners' on his wall, its brilliant colours turn into lustreless ochre and sepia, sombre browns and blues. The critic has made a victim, a young artist whom he condemned as a poor colourist; and when the youth commits suicide, the former must face the truth of the lie he has lived. Through his protagonist,

---

[2] Ricardo Doménech, *El teatro de Antonio Buero Vallejo* (Madrid: Gredos, 1973), p. 49 ff.

who stands for anyone in a position of power, Buero renders a judgement on transition Spain, denouncing the hypocrisy and deception he still sees present after two years of Socialist government.

Buero Vallejo's *Música cercana* (trans. Marion P. Holt *The Music Window*) (1989) features a ruthless executive, Alfredo, whose fortune – from sordid deals of which he feigns ignorance – permits him a life of luxury and privilege. Middle-aged and lonely, he returns to his childhood home, with its window looking onto a courtyard where he hears melodies associated with a girl he once loved. To escape his meaningless life, Alfredo pins his hope on a route that leads, through a symbolic window, to an impossible past – a past that once could have been but was not and that now is impossible to recover. His situation suggests Spanish society in the late 1980s. Behind the bright facade of the economic boom, of a nation of frivolous big spenders and a cult of material success, is the reality evident in the references to alarms, locks and the bodyguards that Alfredo has to follow his daughter. These precautions notwithstanding, the young woman is fatally stabbed in the street by a drug addict. Spain has become another deceptive 'foundation', that is, another prison.

Shortly after Buero Vallejo began his career in 1949, he was joined by another equally committed playwright, Alfonso Sastre. The situation of Alfonso Sastre (b. 1926) in Spanish and world theatre is paradoxical. For much of the Franco period, his works were censored in his homeland while being performed widely abroad. His international reputation far exceeded his impact on the Spanish stage, except through his books of theatre theory. At the advent of democracy, when plays by other prohibited authors were finally produced, Sastre was in prison. He continued to be marginalized until 1985, when he was awarded the National Theatre Prize for *La taberna fantástica* (*The Fantastic Tavern*), a work from 1966 that was given an exciting, hyperrealistic staging by director Gerardo Malla. The doors of the CDN at last opened to Sastre a few years later, but that integration into the official stage immediately preceded the practices that have since tended to exclude living Spanish authors.

Sastre's first major play, the existentialist *Escuadra hacia la muerte* (*The Condemned Squad*) (1953) was closed by official censorship after three performances for its antimilitarism. In the 1950s, he concentrated on a socially-committed Sartrean theatre, centering on revolution and the moral ambiguity of terrorism and violence. He called these dramas criminal investigations into the great social crimes and the collective suffering of his time. By the early 1960s, he abandoned Aristotelian concepts of tragedy and moved to epic theatre. Among his most performed plays in several European countries are *Guillermo Tell tiene los ojos tristes* (*Sad Are the Eyes of William Tell*) (1962), an ironic inversion of the historical tale, and *Historia de una muñeca abandonada* (*Story of an Abandoned Doll*) (1964). This charming reworking as children's theatre of

Brecht's *The Caucasian Chalk Circle* was brilliantly revived in 1989 at the CDN. Dating from the mid-1960s are his 'complex tragedies', which combine elements of classic tragedy with Brechtian techniques and a use of the grotesque reminiscent of Valle-Inclán. Two historical plays from this group, *La sangre y la ceniza* (*Blood and Ashes*) (1967) and *Crónicas romanas* (*Roman Chronicles*) (1970), have been done successfully abroad. *Los últimos días de Emmanuel Kant, contados por Ernesto Teodoro Amadeo Hoffmann* (*The Last Days of Emmanuel Kant, As Told by Ernest Teodoro Amadeo Hoffmann*), a more recent historical play which incorporates elements of the fantastic, was chosen for a major 1990 production at the CDN. The juxtaposition of two planes of reality and overt metatheatricalism present here are, paradoxically, trademark features of this author who is so often associated with Spain's Realistic Generation.

The early 1960s saw the emergence of a new group of playwrights who, like Buero Vallejo and Sastre, cultivated a theatre of 'protest and denunciation': Lauro Olmo (1922–1994), José Martín Recuerda (b. 1925), José María Rodríguez Méndez (b. 1925) and Carlos Muñiz (1927–1994).[3]

It was on the occasion of the opening of Olmo's *La camisa* (*The Shirt*), in 1962, that noted Madrid critic José Monleón first called these playwrights the 'Realistic Generation', underscoring their decidedly critical vision of Franco's Spain.[4] Although their approaches to the theatre vary considerably, they often adapt the popular realism of the brief farce or *sainete*, with its vivid, natural dialogue, music, dance, and local colour, to their social thematics. While Muñiz is best known for his expressionistic allegory, *El tintero* (*The Inkwell*) (1961) all of them emphasize the need for a genuinely popular theatre representative of, and directed to, all of society, rather than the theatre-going middle class. The years immediately following Franco's death saw the staging of many plays of this group that had been previously censored. Indeed, the opening of Martín Recuerda's *Las arrecogías del beaterio de Santa María Egipciaca* (*The Inmates of the Convent of St. Mary Egyptian*) (1977) constituted one of the most notable events in the social and cultural history of post-Civil War Spain.[5]

The beginning of Olmo's career was spectacular. In 1962, *La camisa*, originally scheduled for a single evening, ran for 106 performances at Madrid's Goya Theatre and another hundred at the Maravillas and went on to win the Valle-Inclán, Larra, and National Theatre Awards. In its social criticism, Olmo's drama, set in a shantytown on the city's outskirts, surpassed anything previously seen on the Spanish stage. *La*

---

[3] Francisco Ruiz Ramón, *Historia del teatro español. Siglo XX* (Madrid: Catedra, 1975), p. 485.
[4] José Monleón, 'Nuestra generación realista', *Primer Acto*, no. 32, 1962, pp. 1–13.
[5] Robert Nicholas, *El sainete serio* (Murcia: Universidad de Murcia, 1992), p. 11.

camisa focuses on two major problems of the 1960s: unemployment and the emigration of Spanish workers to find jobs in the industrialized nations of northern Europe. Olmo's characters dream of winning the football pools or of emigrating – topics of avid discussion in the bar where they meet to escape the squalour of their hovels. The dilemma of whether to remain in their own country, where they were convinced that they had a right to be able to work, or to leave for exile was a problem shared by both shantytown dwellers and intellectuals during the Franco years. Juan's conviction that it is in Spain where the real solution must be found reflects the personal stance of Olmo, Buero, and other committed dramatists who stayed in their native land. *La camisa* is much more than a play about Spain's poor and their lost dreams and illusions; the hope expressed in the work is universal. The play has been performed in Frankfurt, Geneva, Paris, Buenos Aires, São Paulo, and other cities, often in the original by workers who had emigrated from Spain.

Beginning in 1965, Olmo began to compose the sort of brief plays that constitute his most original contribution. His collection, *El cuarto poder* (*The Fourth Estate*) – which he calls a 'tragicomic kaleidoscope' – deals with the power of the press and its management of the news. Olmo conceived the collection as an open-ended repertoire in which the composition could be constantly varied, as a living newspaper that could gradually replace his own pieces with those of other writers, national and international.

The year 1986 saw the première in Madrid's Centro Cultural de la Villa of Olmo's *La jerga nacional* (*National Jargon*), a collection of mini-tragicomedies satirizing Spain of the transition period. The setting for all is El Café Español. Spain is a café that different persons enter and leave, and the various plays are strung together with popular songs and dances.

Long one of the most beloved and admired figures in Spain's theatre world, Olmo died in 1994. Of all the playwrights of his generation, he was the one most adversely affected by government censorship, which prevented the staging of many of his works in the Franco era. He was subsequently ignored during the Transition by producers who wanted to be politically correct.

Like García Lorca, Martín Recuerda has sought his inspiration in the towns and villages of his native Andalusia. Recuerda portrays a violently tragic Andalusia with all its sexual repression, fear, cruelty, and hatred – an Andalusia totally opposed to the sunny, joyful, and euphoric place advertised to tourists.

Recuerda's most successful plays to date are *Las salvajes en Puente San Gil* (*The Savages in Puente San Gil*) (1963) and *Las arrecogías del beaterio de Santa María Egipciaca* (*The Inmates of the Convent of Saint Mary Egyptian*) (1977). Representative of Recuerda's increasingly violent, frenzied, and paroxysmal theatre, *Las salvajes en Puente San Gil* builds upon a chain of physical confrontations. When a company of chorus girls arrives in a provincial town to put on a review, they are denounced to the ecclesiastical authorities by the intransigently puritanical wives of the town authorities, attacked brutally by village youths, and used by the town officials to satisfy their own aggressive and ill-repressed sexuality. As the actresses are led off to a police van, they refuse to be silenced and raise their voices defiantly in a song of protest. Martín Recuerda's drama provoked a scandal at the time of its première but, in a modified version, was made into a popular movie in the 1960s and in 1983 was presented in a new television version. In 1985, some twenty-five years after the polemical opening of the censored version, the play went on tour throughout Spain, prior to a successful Madrid revival.[6]

Las arrecogías del beaterio de Santa María Egipciaca focuses on the last day in the life of Mariana Pineda, a Grenadine martyr in the cause of freedom in nineteenth-century Spain. Recuerda emphasizes Mariana's relevance to Spain in the 1970s. As narrators – a chorus of young seamstresses – wander throughout the theatre singing and dancing, stage and house merge and the 1830s become the 1970s. In accord with the collective emphasis of his theatre, Recuerda postulates the existence of other political prisoners, inventing a group of women whose stories, although fictional, are no less significant than Mariana's own. The playwright merges the fate of Mariana and her sister prisoners with that of the audience through the use of songs of resistance. At one climactic moment the chorus of prisoners in the convent sings of the liberals expected to rescue them, and the seamstresses sing and dance in the theatre aisles. Then, Mariana and the other inmates, still singing, come down from the stage to the house aisles as bars descend from the theatre ceiling, turning the spectators into prisoners. The example of Mariana, who goes to her death rather than reveal the names of other conspirators against the tyrannical Ferdinand VII, and of her sister prisoners was relevant to 1977, when ETA members awaited trial in Spain's prisons. The play became a cry for amnesty and freedom and its opening marked the virtual end to four decades of government censorship of the theatre. An English version of *Las arrecogías del beaterio de Santa María Egipciaca* was performed by the Oxford Theatre Group at the 1988 Edinburgh Festival.

El engañao (The Man Who Was Deceived) (1981), which was written in 1972 and won for its author an unprecedented second Lope de Vega Prize,

---

[6] The story was based on Martín Recuerda's observation while touring Southern Spain as director of the University of Granada Theatre Group for seven years. See Ángel Cobo, *José Martín Recuerda: Génesis y evolución de un autor dramático* (Granada: Diputación de Granada, 1993), pp. 65–66.

likewise employs distancing to present problems of twentieth-century Spain. Recuerda's new victims are Juan de Dios or John of God (the man deceived), and the wounded soldiers and deserters he shelters in his hospital – victims of the foreign policy of Hapsburg Carlos V.

Las Conversiones (The Conversions), which opened in 1983 with the title Carnaval de un reino (Carnival of a Kingdom), completes Martín Recuerda's trilogy of history plays. Set in fifteenth-century Castile during the time of Enrique de Trastamara (known as 'The Impotent'), fratricidal wars over the throne, the persecution of the Jews that inspired terror throughout Castile, and a general subversion of human values, the work is the playwright's homage to Castile, especially Salamanca, where he headed the university's theatre department for many years. The Salamanca performance far eclipsed the Madrid opening, in which González Vergel used cross-gender casting to underscore the idea of carnival, and pointed to the importance of the new regional playhouses. Of the members of the 'Realistic Generation' Martín Recuerda has enjoyed the greatest commercial success by far, despite the polemics which his plays have often inspired.

Nowhere is the reality of Franco's Spain portrayed with more bitterness and anger than in the dramas of Rodríguez Méndez. The roots of Rodríguez Méndez's theatre lie in the popular realism of Cervantes and the picaresque novel, the black humour of Goya, the esperpento, and the sainete and género chico, or short plays that appeared at the end of the nineteenth century as a reaction against bourgeois drama.

Rodríguez Méndez's dominant theme is the tragedy of Spanish youth and their frustrated idealism. In his early naturalistic Vagones de madera (Wooden Train Cars) (1959) he showed the fate of young soldiers carted off in 1921 to serve as cannon fodder in the senseless colonial war in North Africa. Los inocentes de la Moncloa (The Innocents of Moncloa) (1961), a key example of the critical realism of the 1960s, presents a picture of student life and an acerbic denunciation of the oposiciones, or public examinations, required to obtain professional-level positions in Spain.

Rodríguez Méndez's most significant dramas are his more recent social chronicles, which depict various moments in Spain's history – both past and present – as seen through the eyes of the common people. Historia de unos cuantos (Story of a Few People), written in 1971 and premiered in 1976, depicts the lives of two families throughout a half-century of Spain's history. The staging of plays by members of the 'Realistic Generation' that followed Franco's death, which started with Rodríguez Méndez's Historia de unos cuantos, continued with his Bodas que fueron famosas del Pingajo y la Fandanga (The Famous Nuptials of Pingajo and Fandanga). The play, written in 1965, was chosen to open the CDN's Bellas Artes Theatre in the fall of 1978. The action is set in 1898 in a poor district of Madrid. Strongly antimilitaristic, the play chronicles the exploits of a ragged scarecrow soldier, who has just returned from the war in Cuba, and his innocent child bride. Long censored, the drama contains numerous passages ridiculing the Army – an untouchable institution in the Franco era.

Flor de Otoño (*Autumn Flower*), written in 1972 and not staged until 1982 in Madrid's Teatro Español, was inspired by the picture from an old chronicle of a transvestite singer of Barcelona's redlight district who was also an anarchist gunman. This historical play effectively recreates Barcelona of the 1930s, from the respectable middle-class society to which the singer belongs, to the Barrio Chino where he performs under his alias, to the workers' cooperatives where the aborted anarchist revolution occurs. The performance, which included cabaret songs in the theatre house as the spectators arrived, was directed by Antonio Díaz Zamora, who had won considerable praise for his production of Martín Recuerda's *Los salvajes en Puente San Gil* in 1963.

In 1985 Rodríguez Méndez's dramatic monologue, *Teresa de Avila*, was performed by the admired actress, María Paz Ballesteros, in Madrid's Capilla del Arzobispo. It was followed four years later by another dramatic monologue, his *El Cantar de los cantares* (*The Song of Songs*), a 'Semitic Oratory for Peace', which opened at the Albéniz Theatre under the sponsorship of the INAEM and the Autonomous Government of Madrid. A single actress played the role of two women representing Palestinians and Jews. As Part I ('Death') opens, the first woman, veiled in black, searches for her children amidst desolation, as a Voice off-stage documents recent struggles between the two peoples. Part II ('Resurrection') is based on the Spanish poet, Luis de León's translation of the Song of Songs. As the Palestinian woman listens to the verses, the emphasis changes from death and destruction to love and resurrection. The actress removes her black shrouds to reveal the red and gold garments of the Biblical Shulammite – the Jewish woman of peace in Rodríguez Méndez's oratory – and the tombstone seen in Part I becomes a banquet table prepared for a celebration.

In 1994 Rodríguez Méndez won the National Theatre Prize for *El pájaro solitario* (*The Solitary Bird*), his play on San Juan de la Cruz (St. John of the Cross). He is also the author of three polemical books of theatre criticism that evince their author's acerbic wit and reflect the bitter experiences of his generation of playwrights.

In the 1960s there emerged in Spain a group of experimental playwrights whose absurdist tragicomedies and political allegories were anti-realistic and non-representational, in apparent opposition in form if not in ideology to the Realistic Generation. Their so-called underground or silenced theatre expressed a deepening anger and fear about the situation in their country and, more generally, about the human condition in our contemporary world. José María Bellido, Angel García

Pintado, Antonio Martínez Ballesteros, Manuel Martínez Mediero, Luis Matilla, Eduardo Quiles, Luis Riaza, José Ruibal, and Alfonso Vallejo, among others, won prizes at festivals in Sitges and elsewhere, were 'discovered' by American scholars, and were performed in the United States and Great Britain; but their works were to go largely unstaged and unknown on the mainstream Spanish stage during the Franco period. Nor, with few exceptions, have they achieved any notable success in democratic Spain.

Of this group only Martínez Mediero (b. 1939) has had box office hits; his satirical allegory on the end of the Franco era, *Las hermanas de Búfalo Bill* (*Buffalo Bill's Sisters*) (1975), ushered in the theatre of transition. His next successful play was a demythologizing, expressionistic, historical tragicomedy about Juana la Loca, *Juana del amor hermoso* (Trans. Hazel Cazorla, *A Love Too Beautiful*) (1983). In the late 1970s, the newly-established CDN, in its short-lived efforts to promote living Spanish authors, did stage memorable productions of *Ejercicios para equilibristas* (*Exercises for Tightrope Walkers*), metaphorical short pieces by Matilla (b. 1939) and *Retrato de dama con perrito* (*Portrait of a Lady with Lapdog*), a Genet-style metaplay by Riaza (b. 1925), but by 1984 official productions of experimental theatre had been shifted to the fringe Sala Olimpia, home of the Centro Nacional de Nuevas Tendencias Escénicas (National Centre for New Tendencies of the Stage). Performances there often played before near empty houses, and in the 1994 reshuffling of government-subsidized theatres, the experimental centre was, at least temporarily, disbanded.

Internationally, Spain's most famous avant-garde writer is undoubtedly Fernando Arrabal (b. 1932), whose residence in France since the 1950s has facilitated his access to theatres around the world. Even today he and his works remain controversial in his native land, although he is much staged by independent groups.

Oye, patria, mi aflicción, rejected by the Spanish censor in 1975, had its world premiere in Belgium in 1976 under its French title, *La Tour de Babel* (*The Tower of Babel*). It is the text with which Arrabal, under Lavelli's direction, entered the repertoire of the Comédie Française in 1979–1980. There is a distinct irony in the greater acclaim it has received in the French-speaking world, for in many ways, it is one of the most 'Spanish' of Arrabal's works. The oneiric, sometimes violent, sometimes comic, action of the sixteen scenes takes place in an isolated, termite-infested castle that, in its obvious decadence, stands as a metaphor for Spain. The characters, drawn primarily from Spanish history and literature, form tableaux and speak lines rich in intertextuality. Arrabal's metatheatrical tour de force, *El Arquitecto y el Emperador de Asiria* (*The Architect and the Emperor of Assyria*), deemed by some to be his masterwork, received its world premiere under Lavelli's inspired direction in 1967 but did not reach the Madrid stage until 1983. Although these two Madrid productions met with positive critical and audience response, their openings at the relatively small Teatro Martín both came in late May, at the end of the theatre season.

The staging of Arrabal's *El rey de Sodoma* (*The King of Sodom*) by the CDN, also in late May of 1983, is unusual in terms of the playwright's presence on the official Spanish stage. On the other hand, his novels circulate widely in Spain, and in 1986, the man who was *persona non grata* during the Franco regime, received a gold medal for achievement in the fine arts from King Juan Carlos.

Another figure of international stature connected with the Spanish stage and popular with independent groups is Jorge Díaz (b. 1930). Born in Argentina, considered to be the first exponent of absurdist theatre in Chile, and certainly one of the outstanding figures of contemporary Latin American theatre, Díaz in fact has lived much of the time in Madrid since the late 1960s. In Madrid he wrote the definitive version of his much admired *El cepillo de dientes* (*The Toothbrush*) (1966). Paradoxically, although he has won a number of prizes in Spain, Díaz has not achieved box office success in his adoptive country.

Within Spain the most visible and successful proponent of anti-realistic, non-representational theatre is unquestionably Francisco Nieva (b. 1927), member of the Spanish Royal Academy who in 1992 became the first playwright to be awarded the prestigious Príncipe de Asturias prize for literature. After years of residence in France and extended stays in Italy and Germany, Nieva returned to Spain in the late 1960s to become his nation's most distinguished stage designer. In the early 1950s he began writing original plays in a surrealist, theatricalist vein – closely related to the international current that Gloria Orenstein has called the Theatre of the Marvelous –[7] but he did not achieve professional productions of any of his works until after Franco's death. His theatre is noted for its verbal and visual imagination and for its spirit of transgression; his plays are highly metatheatrical, often erotic, and always wildly funny.

The staging together in 1976 of *El combate de Opalos y Tasia* (*The Battle of Opalos and Tasia*), an erotic farce that parodies Spanish baroque literature, and *La carroza de plomo candente* (*The Carriage of White-Hot Lead*), a 'black ritual' whose satire focuses on an impotent king, brought Nieva national fame, critical recognition, and the Mayte, the first of several major theatre prizes he was to receive. Other highly praised productions followed during the next several years, some of them designed and directed by the author himself. These successes include a

---

[7] Gloria Orenstein, *The Theatre of the Marvelous: Surrealism and the Contemporary Stage* (New York: New York University Press, 1975).

visually brilliant adaptation of Cervantes's *Los baños de Argel* (*The Baths of Algiers*) (1979); *La señora Tártara* (*Woman from the Nether Land*) (1980), an apocalyptic, whimsical work that introduces an androgynous figure of Death; and *Coronada y el toro* (*Coronada and the Bull*) (1982), a satirical 'Spanish rhapsody' that pokes fun at *machismo* by directing our sympathies toward the female victim of a sexist society, a divine male nun and a reluctant bullfighter.

An anomaly to the pattern of lacklustre productions at the National Centre for New Tendencies of the Stage was Guillermo Heras's dazzling staging in 1993 of *Aquelarre y noche roja de Nosferatu* (*The Witches' Sabbath and Nosferatu's Red Night*), a riotously imaginative play written in 1961. The production emphasized elaborate visual effects, music, and choreographed movement of the actors. The intertext – a 1922 German vampire movie – was projected on a background screen to mark the beginning of each act.

In the 1990s, Nieva has acquired visibility in the national theatres of Paris. During a 1992 series of professional staged readings of Hispanic plays at the Petit Odéon and the Théâtre National de la Colline, his *Baile de los ardientes* (*Dance of the Passionate*) was included in the cycles at both theatres. The enthusiastic reception to that text led to his inclusion in the 1994–1995 season at the Colline. Under the title *Retable des damnées* (*Triptych of the Damned*), a trilogy of Nieva's parodic tales of fantasy, terror and humour, were staged from mid May to late June.

A number of playwrights, of various theatrical tendencies, who entered the Spanish stage in the 1960s, continue to be performed and have developed loyal audiences. Some of these – for example, Juan José Alonso Millán (b. 1938), longtime president of the Sociedad General de Autores de España (Spain's dramatists' guild), and Santiago Moncada (b. 1928), whose *Entre mujeres*, 1988, has been repeatedly staged by Hispanic theatres in the U.S. – favour bourgeois comedy and, probably for that reason, like the prolific Alfonso Paso (1926–1978) before them, are generally overlooked by scholars. Other playwrights, like Jaime Salom (b. 1925), Antonio Gala (b. 1936), and Ana Diosdado (b. 1938), have been the subject of numerous critical studies.

Salom is one of the few Catalan playwrights to become fully integrated into the Madrid stage. Since 1955, he has had some thirty plays staged professionally in Spain, a number of which have been box office hits and won major theatre awards. His first success, *El baúl de los disfraces* (*The Trunk of Disguises*) (1964), is a metatheatrical comedy, but the work that firmly established his fame was an intense, moralistic and psychological drama dealing with individuals behind the lines, on the Republican side, during the Civil War. *La casa de las Chivas* (*The House of the 'Chivas'*) (1968) had a record-breaking run of 1343 performances in a single Madrid playhouse, was made into a movie, and was successfully revived as a television play a decade later.

Starting in the 1970s, Salom's theatre has been marked by constant theatrical experimentation and by an increasingly liberal ideology. *La piel del limón* (Trans. Patricia O'Connor, *Bitter Lemon*) (1976) introduced fluidity of time and space in an expressionistic mode to plea eloquently for divorce reform. Other notable plays include the historical dramas *El corto vuelo del gallo* (*The Cock's Short Flight*) (1980) and *Las Casas. Una hoguera al amanecer* (*Bonfire at Dawn*) (1990). The protagonist of the former is the liberal, libertine father of General Franco, while the latter gives a sensitive, complex and, from the Spanish point of view, controversial portrait of Bartolomé de las Casas. Not only does the play point out the cruelty and greed of some of the Spanish participants in the conquest of the New World, it also suggests that the great defender of the indigenous people was partially motivated to act on their behalf because of the homosexual attraction he had felt for a young Indian. As yet unstaged in Spain, the 'Las Casas' play premiered in Mexico in 1990 and was staged at the GALA Hispanic Theatre in Washington, D.C. in 1992; it has also been made into a movie in Mexico and been performed in France. Several of Salom's plays have been translated into French and been staged in Paris or Toulouse.

The Andalusian Gala, who enjoys celebrity status in Spain, does not consider himself a playwright *per se*; he has written and appeared in television series, has a regular weekly newspaper column, and is also a novelist and poet. His fame as a dramatist dates from the triumphant première in 1963 of his first play, *Los verdes campos del Edén* (*The Green Fields of Eden*). Following the relative failure of other productions in the 1960s, Gala has had a long string of box office hits. His theatre generally blends sparkling surface humour with an underlying tragic reality and tends to function metaphorically. His protagonists typically seek a paradise of political and personal freedom. They champion the cause of the disempowered: women, Jews, homosexuals. Almost invariably Gala's idealists are doomed to failure; exceptions are *Petra Regalada* (1980), an allegory on the end of the Franco era, and *La Truhana* (*The Comedienne*) (1992), a sparkling historical play built on the structures of Golden Age comedy.

Gala's *Los buenos días perdidos* (Trans. Edward Borsoi, *The Bells of Orleans*) (1972), a metaphorical satire of contemporary materialism, was successfully revived in Madrid in 1991. *Anillos para una dama* (*Rings for a Lady*) (1973) is an anachronistic, feminist demystification of the Cid myth, from the perspective of his widow Jimena; it enjoyed a major Madrid revival in 1982. Recent works include the long-running musical *Carmen Carmen* (1988), and the opera libretto *Cristóbal Colón* (*Christopher*

Columbus) (1989). As a featured production of the 1992 Quincentennial, the opera – with music by Leonardo Balada and starring José Carreras – toured internationally.

In the contemporary period, Diosdado is unquestionably the woman author who has had the longest successful career, dating back to the critical and box office triumph of her first play, *Olvida los tambores* (*Forget the Drums*) (1970); this look at divergent life styles and lingering conservative/liberal conflicts won her the Mayte theatre prize. *Usted también podra disfrutar de ella* (Trans. Patricia O'Connor, *Yours for the Asking*) (1973) combines impeccable theatrical structure and sparkling dialogue with an underlying criticism of political divisiveness and materialism.

In spite of these early successes and the visibility achieved through television series in which Diosdado has functioned as both author and actress, like many playwrights in democratic Spain, she has had a difficult time being staged. After a ten-year absence from the stage, she formed her own company in 1986 to bring *Cuplé* (*Ballad*) to audiences. This tragicomic satire of economic problems in contemporary Spain introduced a series of box office hits, the most successful of which has been *Los ochenta son nuestros* (*The Eighties Are Ours*) (1988). Focusing on young people and their search for self-identity, the play also continues Diosdado's typical deconstruction of binary oppositions by exploring prejudice based on ideology, class, and sexual orientation.

Among the first new playwrights to gain national recognition in democratic Spain are José Luis Alonso de Santos (b. 1942) and Fermín Cabal (b. 1948). Although both had been active in independent theatre groups, they were unknown to many Madrid playgoers until the 1982 stagings at the CDN's María Guerrero Theatre of the former's expressionistic and quasi-autobiographical *Album de familia* (*Family Album*) and the latter's *¡Vade retro!* (Trans. Robert Sheehan, *Get Thee Behind Me!*), which portrays a night of verbal battle between two priests of different generations. The following year, Cabal secured his reputation with the success of *¡Esta noche gran velada!* (*Big Match Tonight!*), a hyperrealistic portrayal of the boxing world that is nevertheless marked by comic dialogue, intertextual references to American boxing films, and metatheatrical elements. Cabal's works are beginning to attract international attention, including productions in France.

Among Alonso de Santos's most important works to date, both of which have been made into films, are *La estanquera de Vallecas* (Trans. Zatlin *Hostages in the Barrio*) (1981), and *Bajarse al moro* (Trans. Zatlin *Going Down to Marrakesh*), winner of the National Theatre Prize for 1985. Typically Alonso de Santos's plays are bittersweet comedies. Their surface humour, creative use of contemporary slang, and intertextual references to filmic codes make them particularly appealing to a younger generation of theatre-goers.

While Salom has long been the most successful Catalan playwright on the Madrid stage, in the 1990s other authors residing in Barcelona have been staged by national theatres in the capital. Historical dramas about Lope de Aguirre by José Sanchis Sinisterra (b. 1940) were showcased in government-subsidized theatre projects related to the Quincentennial. Sinisterra's selection was no doubt influenced by the enormous success of his *¡Ay, Carmela!* (1987), a two-character metaplay about the Spanish Civil War that was made into a hit movie and has been staged in England and France. Sergi Belbel (b. 1963) writes in Catalan and is a young playwright who has recently received official support. His *Tálem* (*Matrimonial Bed*) received its première in Castilian at the National Centre for New Tendencies of the Stage in 1991, and *Carícies* (*Caresses*) was the text chosen by Guillermo Heras as the final production of that centre in 1994. The first centres on a married couple's sexual problems, while the latter, built on the structure of Schnitzler's *La Ronde*, presents an interlocking chain of couples. Both works were also chosen for staged readings in the 1992 Hispanic cycles in Paris.

In the past decade, other women writers have joined Diosdado on the Madrid stage. The most commercially successful of these is unquestionably María Manuela Reina (b. 1958) although Paloma Pedrero (b. 1957) has achieved the greatest international recognition, with stagings in England, France, Brazil, Portugal and the United States. Many women playwrights still find it difficult to have their works staged at all; even prize-winning works are not immediately performed, if ever. The women dramatists created their own association as a support group in 1987, under the presidency of Carmen Resino (b. 1941). Some, like Resino, Pilar Pombo (b. 1953) and Concha Romero (b. 1945), have turned at times to writing dramatic monologues which can be produced inexpensively in nontraditional playing spaces.

Reina's *Lutero o la libertad esclava* (*Luther or Freedom Enslaved*), winner of the Calderón de la Barca prize for 1984 and staged at Madrid's Centro Cultural de la Villa in 1987, is an imaginary, philosophical dialogue between Luther and Erasmus. Her more recent works – notably *La cinta dorada* (*Gold Ribbon*) (1988), and *Reflejos con cenizas* (*Reflections with Ashes*) (1991) – are conventional bourgeois dramas dealing with dysfunctional families and taboo sexual relationships; they enjoy long runs in commercial playhouses.

Pedrero won the 1987 Tirso de Molina prize for *Invierno de luna alegre* (*Winter's Happy Moon*), which she directed in 1989. That view of marginal members of society, including an ex-bullfighter who earns his living by staging street spectacles, calls for a cast of five; but thus far Pedrero's most-staged works are her intimate, intense, two-character plays which capture moments of crisis in self-identity or relationships. *La llamada de Lauren* (*Lauren's Call*) reveals the problems of a young married couple resulting from the husband's ambivalence about his sexual identity; Pedrero herself played Rosa in the 1985 Madrid premiere at the Centro Cultural de la Villa. *El color de agosto* (*The Color of August*) (1988) portrays the artistic and personal rivalries of two women artists, who have been friends since childhood but are reunited after an eight-year separation.

Pedrero is among the younger playwrights who, in contrast to the emphasis on theatrical spectacle of collective groups in recent years, has once again focused on the verbal text.[8] As O'Connor has noted, their well-made plays tend to be realistic and to reflect the latest language of the streets.[9] Their theatre is often humorous and makes reference to the cultural interests of a young audience. Many of their works are short and are written for a small cast, thus facilitating performance. Other playwrights in this generation, born in the late 1950s and early 1960s, are Ernesto Caballero, Eduardo Galán, Ignacio García May, Ignacio del Moral, Antonio Onetti, and Alfonso Plou.

Theatre in Spain always seems to be in crisis, but it has managed to survive the challenges, be they economic, political or cultural. At the start of the 1994–1995 season, Cristina Ferreiro reported to *Estreno* an encouraging number of major productions of new works by living authors: Buero Vallejo's *Las trampas del azar* (*The Traps of Fate*), Gala's *Los bellos durmientes* (*Sleeping Beauties*), Diosdado's *Cristal de bohemia* (*Bohemian Crystal*), Sastre's *¿Dónde estás, Ululame, dónde estás?* (*Where Are You, Ululame, Where Are You?*), Moncada's *Mejor en octubre* (*It's Better in October*), Alonso de Santos's *Horas de visita* (*Visiting Hours*) and *La sombra del Tenorio* (*Don Juan's Shadow*), and Sanchis Sinisterra's *El Cerco de Leningrado* (*The Siege of Leningrad*).[10] The number and variety of these recent plays offers hope for the future of the Spanish stage and proves, once again, that there is life after Lorca.

References

Alonso de Santos. *Going Down to Marrakesh*. Trans. Phyllis Zatlin. In *Plays of the New Democratic Spain* (1975–1990). Ed. Patricia W. O'Connor. Lanham, New York and London: University Press of America, 1992, pp. 313–379

Alonso de Santos. *Hostages in the Barrio*. Trans. Phyllis Zatlin. University Park, PA: Estreno, forthcoming

---

[8] The contemporary Catalan stage has produced a number of innovative groups – for example, Els Joglars, Els Comediants, La Fura dels Baus, Tricicle – that have toured internationally to great acclaim. A discussion of their work falls outside the scope of this overview, which has concentrated on individual authors and theatre in Madrid.

[9] Patricia O'Conner, 'The *Primer Grupo de la Democracia* and the Return to the Word', *Estreno*, 17, no. 1, 1991, p. 13.

[10] Cristina Ferreiro, 'Cartelera', *Estreno*, 21, no. 1, 1995, p. 60.

Arrabal, Fernando. *The Architect and the Emperor of Assyria*. Trans. Everard d'Harnoncourt and Adele Shank. New York: Grove Press, 1969

Buero Vallejo, Antonio. *The Basement Window*. Trans. Patricia W. O'Connor. In *Plays of Protest from the Franco Era*. Madrid: SGEL, 1981, pp. 15–106

Buero Vallejo. *The Concert at Saint Ovide*. Trans. Farris Anderson. *Modern International Drama*, 1, no. 1, September 1967, pp. 6–61

Buero Vallejo. *The Double Case History of Doctor Valmy*. Trans. Farris Anderson. *Artes Hispánicas*, 1, no. 1, Autumn 1967, pp. 85–169

Buero Vallejo. *A Dreamer for the People*. Trans. Michael Thompson. Warminster, England: Aries & Phillips, 1993

Buero Vallejo. *The Foundation*. Trans. Marion P. Holt. In *Antonio Buero-Vallejo: Three Plays*. San Antonio, TX: Trinity University Press, 1985, pp. 59–133

Buero Vallejo. *Las Meninas*. Trans. Marion P. Holt. San Antonio, TX: Trinity University Press, 1987

Buero Vallejo. *The Music Window*. Trans. Marion P. Holt. University Park, PA: Estreno, 1994

Buero Vallejo. *The Sleep of Reason*. Trans. Marion P. Holt. In *Antonio Buero-Vallejo: Three Plays*. San Antonio, TX: Trinity University Press, 1985, pp. 2–58

Cabal, Fermín. *Get Thee Behind Me!*. Trans. Robert Sheehan. *Estreno*, 14, no. 2, 1988, pp. 14–29

Diosdado, Ana. *Yours for the Asking*. Trans. Patricia W. O'Connor. University Park, PA: Estreno, 1995

Gala, Antonio. *The Bells of Orleans*. Trans. Edward Borsoi. University Park, PA: Estreno, 1993

Gala, Antonio. *The Green Fields of Eden*. Trans. Patricia W. O'Connor. In *Contemporary Spanish Theatre: The Social Comedies of the Sixties*. Madrid: SGEL, 1983, pp. 189–254

Jardiel Poncela, Enrique. *Eloise Is Under an Almond Tree*. Trans. Steven Capsuto. In *Plays of the New Democratic Spain* (1975–1990). Ed. Patricia W. O'Connor. Lanham, New York and London: University Press of America, 1992, pp. 1–102

López Rubio, José. *The Blindfold*. Trans. Marion P. Holt. In *The Modern Spanish Stage: Four Plays*. New York: Hill and Wang, 1970, pp 211–313

López Rubio, José. *In August We Play the Pyrenees*. Trans. Marion P. Holt. University Park, PA: Estreno, 1992

Martín Recuerda, José. *The Inmates of the Convent of St. Mary Egyptian*. Trans. Robert Lima. In *Drama Contemporary: Spain*. Ed. Marion P. Holt. New York: Performing Arts Journal Publications, 1985, pp. 97–138

Martínez Mediero, Manuel. *A Love Too Beautiful*. Trans. Hazel Cazorla. University Park, PA: Estreno, 1995

Mihura, Miguel. *Three Top Hats*. Trans. Marcia Cobourn Wellwarth. In *Modern Spanish Theatre*. Ed. George Wellwarth. New York: E. P. Dutton and Company, 1968. pp. 127–194

Muñiz, Carlos. *The Inkwell*. Trans. Patricia W. O'Connor. In *Plays of Protest from the Franco Era*. Madrid: SGEL, 1981, pp. 175–250

Nieva, Francisco. *The Carriage of White-Hot Lead*. Trans. Emil Signes. Ph.D. dissertation, Rutgers, 1982

Nieva, Francisco. *Coronada and the Bull*. Trans. Emil Signes. In *Drama Contemporary: Spain*. Ed. Marion P. Holt. New York: Performing Arts Journal Publications, 1985, pp. 191–229

Olmo, Lauro. *The Shirt*. Trans. Patricia W. O'Connor. In *Plays of Protest from the Franco Era*. Madrid: SGEL, 1981, pp. 103–174

Pedrero, Paloma. *The Color of August*. In *Parting Gestures*. Trans. Phyllis Zatlin. University Park, PA: Estreno, 1994

Salom, Jaime. *Bitter Lemon*. Trans. Patricia W. O'Connor. In *Plays of the New Democratic Spain* (1975–1990). Ed. Patricia W. O'Connor. Lanham, New York and London: University Press of America, 1992, pp. 103–164

Salom, Jaime. *Bonfire at Dawn*. Trans. Phyllis Zatlin. University Park, PA: Estreno, 1992

Salom, Jaime. *The Cock's Short Flight*. Trans. Marion P. Holt. In *Drama Contemporary*: Spain. Ed. Marion P. Holt. New York: Performing Arts Journal Publications, 1985, pp. 139–190

Sastre, Alfonso. *The Condemned Squad*. Trans. Leonard C. Pronko. In *The Modern Spanish Stage: Four Plays*. New York: Hill and Wang, 1970, pp. 139–203

Sastre, Alfonso. *Sad Are the Eyes of William Tell*. In *The New Wave Spanish Drama*. Ed. George E. Wellwarth. New York: New York University Press, 1970, pp 265–321

Sastre, Alfonso. *Story of an Abandoned Doll*. Trans. Carys Evans-Corrales. University Park, PA: Estreno, 1996. Forthcoming

Valle-Inclán, Ramón María del. *Divine Words. A Village Tragicomedy*. Trans. Maria M. Delgado. *Valle-Inclán Plays: One*. London: Methuen, 1993, pp. 1–89. Additional contents: *Bohemian Lights*, pp. 91–184, *Silver Face*, pp. 185–273

Valle-Inclán, Ramón María del. *Lights of Bohemia*. Trans. Anthony N. Zahareas and Gerald Gillespie. *Modern International Drama*, 2, no. 2, 1969, pp. 53–97

Contemporary Theatre Review
1998, Vol. 7, Part 2, pp. 81–82
Reprints available directly from the publisher
Photocopying permitted by license only

Notes on Contributors

Maria M. Delgado is a lecturer in Drama at Queen Mary and Westfield College, the University of London. She is co-editor of the recent *In contact with the gods?: Directors talk theatre* (Manchester: Manchester University Press, 1996), and editor of *Valle-Inclán Plays: One* (London: Methuen, 1993). She is author of numerous articles on Hispanic and British theatre and Spanish film, co-programmer of the Manchester Spanish Film Festival, a Drama Advisor for North West Arts, and an advisor to the London film festival. She is currently working on two books with the American director Peter Sellars.

Martha T. Halsey is Emeritus Professor of Spanish at the The Pennsylvania State University. She has prepared editions of plays by Buero Vallejo, Ródriguez Méndez and Martín Recuerda, and is author of the recent *From Dictatorship to Democracy: The Recent Plays of Antonio Buero Vallejo (From 'La Fundación' to 'Música cercana')*. In 1980 she organized an international symposium on contemporary Spanish theatre and she has been editor of *Estreno* since 1992. In 1996 she was elected an Honorary Research fellow of The Hispanic Society of America.

Robert Lima has published widely as a poet, translator, critic, biographer and bibliographer. Amongst his books are the poetry collections *Fathoms, The Olde Ground,* and *Mayaland;* the now classic critical study *The Theatre of García Lorca,* and *Borges the Labyrinth Maker* (edited and translated), the first assessment in English on the noted Argentine author. His books on Valle-Inclán include *Ramón del Valle-Inclán, An Annotated Bibliography of Valle-Inclán, Dos ensayos sobre teatro español de los veinte* (co-authored), the translation of *The Lamp of Marvels,* and the first biography on the subject in English, *Valle-Inclán, The Theatre of His Life.* His latest book is *Dark Prisms, Occultism in Hispanic Drama.* His biography of Valle-Inclán has been published in Spanish translation in 1995 by Nigra Imaxe, while a new edition of the bibliography, in two volumes, is being issued in 1997 by Grant & Cutler Ltd. in London. He is Professor of Spanish and Comparative Literature, as well as Fellow of the Institute for the Arts and Humanistic Studies, at The Pennsylvania State University.

James McCarthy is a lecturer in Drama at Trinity College, Camarthen where he teaches courses in performance and modern British drama.

José A. Sánchez is Dean of the Faculty of Fine Arts at the University of Castilla la Mancha in Cuenca, where he teaches the History of Contemporary Theatre and Contemporary Art and Literature. He has published two books, *Brecht y el Expresionismo* (Brecht and Expressionism) and *Dramaturgias de la imagen* (Dramaturgies of images), and several articles on aesthetics and theatre criticism. He has worked as dramaturg and director at the University Theatre Group in Murcia and with the professional company E.A.T. With these groups he has adapted and directed works by Julio Cortázar, García Lorca, Ernst Toller, and Gómez de la Serna, amongst others. He now directs the Laboratory of Scenic Arts in the Faculty of Fine Arts in Cuenca.

Phyllis Zatlin is Professor and director of translator training in the Department of Spanish at Rutgers University. She is author of books on the theatre of Ruiz Iriarte and Salom as well as of the recent *Cross-Cultural Approaches to Theatre: The Spanish-French Connection*, 1994, and editor of plays by Ruiz Iriarte, Salom, Gala, and Nieva. Her translations of plays by Salom, Pedrero, and Alonso de Santos have been published and have received recent American premieres. She has been Associate Editor of *Estreno* since 1992.

Contemporary Theatre Review
1998, Vol. 7, Part 2, pp. 83–86
Reprints available directly from the publisher
Photocopying permitted by license only

Index

Play titles are listed by author and films are listed by title. Devised pieces are listed under the name of the company or director who produced them. I refer to the main text only and not to the notes.

CONTEMPORARY THEATRE REVIEW
AN INTERNATIONAL JOURNAL

Notes for contributors.

Submission of a paper will be taken to imply that it represents original work not previously published, that it is not being considered for publication elsewhere and that, if accepted for publication, it will not be published elsewhere in the same form, in any language, without the consent of editor and publisher. It is a condition of acceptance by the editor of a typescript for publication that the publisher automatically acquires the copyright of the typescript throughout the world. It will also be assumed that the author has obtained all necessary permissions to include in the paper items such as quotations, musical examples, figures, tables etc. Permissions should be paid for prior to submission.

Typescripts. Papers should be submitted in triplicate to the Editors, *Contemporary Theatre Review*, c/o Harwood Academic Publishers, at:

5th Floor, Reading Bridge House	820 Town Center Drive	3-14-9, Okubo
Reading Bridge Approach or	Langhorne or	Shinjuku-ku
Reading RGl 8PP	PA 19047 USA	Tokyo 169
UK		Japan

Papers should be typed or word processed with double spacing on one side of good quality ISO A4 (212 × 297 mm) paper with a 3 cm left-hand margin. Papers are accepted only in English.

Abstracts and Keywords. Each paper requires an abstract of 100–150 words summarizing the significant coverage and findings, presented on a separate sheet of paper. Abstracts should be followed by up to six key words or phrases which, between them, should indicate the subject matter of the paper. These will be used for indexing and data retrieval purposes.

Figures. All figures (photographs, schema, charts, diagrams and graphs) should be numbered with consecutive arabic numerals, have descriptive captions and be mentioned in the text. Figures should be kept separate from the text but an approximate position for each should be indicated in the margin of the typescript. It is the author's responsibility to obtain permission for any reproduction from other sources.

Preparation: Line drawings must be of a high enough standard for direct reproduction; photocopies are not acceptable. They should be prepared in black (india) ink on white art paper, card or tracing paper, with all the lettering and symbols included. Computer-generated graphics of a similar high quality are also acceptable, as are good sharp photoprints ("glossies"). Computer print-outs must be completely legible. Photographs intended for halftone reproduction must be good glossy original prints of maximum contrast. Redrawing or retouching of unusable figures will be charged to authors.

Size: Figures should be planned so that they reduce to 12 cm column width. The preferred width of line drawings is 24 cm, with capital lettering 4 mm high, for reduction by one-half. Photographs for halftone reproduction should be approximately twice the desired finished size.

Captions: A list of figure captions, with the relevant figure numbers, should be typed on a separate sheet of paper and included with the typescript.

Musical examples: Musical examples should be designated as "Figure 1" etc., and the recommendations above for preparation and sizing should be followed. Examples must be well prepared and of a high standard for reproduction, as they will not be redrawn or retouched by the printer.

In the case of large scores, musical examples will have to be reduced in size and so some clarity will be lost. This should be borne in mind especially with orchestral scores.

Notes are indicated by superior arabic numerals without parentheses. The text of the notes should be collected at the end of the paper.

References are indicated in the text by the name and date system either "Recent work (Smith & Jones, 1987, Robinson, 1985, 1987) . . ." or "Recently Smith & Jones (1987) . . ." If a publication has more than three authors, list all names on the first occurrence; on subsequent occurrences use the first author's name plus "*et al.*" Use an ampersand rather than "and" between the last two authors. If there is more than one publication by the same author(s) in the same year, distinguish by adding a, b, c etc. to both the text citation and the list of references (e.g. "Smith, 1986a") References should be collected and typed in alphabetical order after the Notes and Acknowledgements sections (if these exist). Examples:

Benedetti, J. (1988) *Stanislavski*, London: Methuen

Granville-Barker, H. (1934) Shakespeare's dramatic art. In *A Companion to Shakespeare Studies*, edited by H. Granville-Barker and G. B. Harrison, p. 84. Cambridge: Cambridge University Press

Johnston, D. (1970) Policy in theatre. *Hibernia*, 16, 16

Proofs. Authors will receive page proofs (including figures) by air mail for correction and these must be returned as instructed within 48 hours of receipt. Please ensure that a full postal address is given on the first page of the typescript so that proofs are not delayed in the post. Authors' alterations, other than those of a typographical nature, in excess of 10% of the original composition cost, will be charged to authors.

Page Charges. There are no page charges to individuals or institutions.

INSTRUCTIONS FOR AUTHORS

ARTICLE SUBMISSION ON DISK

The Publisher welcomes submissions on disk. The instructions that follow are intended for use by authors whose articles have been accepted for publication and are in final form. Your adherence to these guidelines will facilitate the processing of your disk by the typesetter. These instructions do not replace the journal Notes for Contributors; all information in Notes for Contributors remains in effect.

When typing your article, do not include design or formatting information. Type all text flush left, unjustified and without hyphenation. Do not use indents, tabs or multi-spacing. If an indent is required, please note it by a line space; also mark the position of the indent on the hard copy manuscript. Indicate the beginning of a new paragraph by typing a line space. Leave one space at the end of a sentence, after a comma or other punctuation mark, and before an opening parenthesis. Be sure not to confuse lower case letter "l" with numeral "1", or capital letter "O" with numeral "0". Distinguish opening quotes from close quotes. Do not use automatic page numbering or running heads.

Tables and displayed equations may have to be rekeyed by the typesetter from your hard copy manuscript. Refer to the journal Notes for Contributors for style for Greek characters, variables, vectors, etc.

Articles prepared on most word processors are acceptable. If you have imported equations and/or scientific symbols into your article from another program, please provide details of the program used and the procedures you followed. If you have used macros that you have created, please include them as well.

You may supply illustrations that are available in an electronic format on a separate disk. Please clearly indicate on the disk the file format and/or program used to produce them, and supply a high-quality hard copy of each illustration as well.

Submit your disk when you submit your final hard copy manuscript. The disk file and hard copy must match exactly.

If you are submitting more than one disk, please number each disk. Please mark each disk with the journal title, author name, abbreviated article title and file names.

Be sure to retain a back-up copy of each disk submitted. Pack your disk carefully to avoid damage in shipping, and submit it with your hard copy manuscript and complete Disk Specifications form (see reverse) to the person designated in the journal Notes for Contributors.

Disk Specifications

Journal name _____

Date _____ **Paper Reference Number** _____

Paper title _____

_____

_____

Corresponding author _____

Address _____

_____

_____

_____ **Postcode** _____

Telephone _____

Fax _____

E-mail _____

Disks Enclosed (file names and descriptions of contents)

Text

Disk 1 _____

Disk 2 _____

Disk 3 _____

PLEASE RETAIN A BACK-UP COPY OF ALL DISK FILES SUBMITTED.

GORDON AND BREACH PUBLISHERS ● **HARWOOD ACADEMIC PUBLISHERS**

Figures

Disk 1 _____

Disk 2 _____

Disk 3 _____

Computer make and model _____

_____

Size/format of floppy disks

☐ 3.5"   ☐ 5.25"

☐ Single sided   ☐ Double sided

☐ Single density   ☐ Double density   ☐ High density

Operating system _____

Version _____

Word processor program _____

Version _____

Imported maths/science program _____

Version _____

Graphics program _____

Version _____

Files have been saved in the following format

Text: _____

Figures: _____

Maths: _____

PLEASE RETAIN A BACK-UP COPY OF ALL DISK FILES SUBMITTED.

GORDON AND BREACH PUBLISHERS   •   **HARWOOD ACADEMIC PUBLISHERS**

Printed in the United Kingdom
by Lightning Source UK Ltd.
124910UK00001B/66/A